PRAISE FOR *THE MINDFUL GRANDPARENT: THE ART OF LOVING OUR CHILDREN'S CHILDREN*

"This is a book I did not know I was waiting for. It is a reflective handbook for becoming a grandparent—perhaps the first ever?—but so much more. A celebration of the flow and fullness of life. A call to the honor and pleasures of eldering. It is a gift to our world which is so in need of—and so ripe for—old ways and new of deep accompaniment and formation across generations."

> —**Krista Tippett**, founder and editor-in-chief of The On Being Project, host of On Being program and podcast, and recipient of the National Humanities Medal

"*The Mindful Grandparent* is not only warm, loving, and practical; it's also gently honest. The authors know that this three-generation dance between grandparents, their own children, and their grandkids sometimes means that toes get stepped on. But as we learn the steps involved in doing a dance, we see more clearly that this three-generation dance is grace-filled."

> —**Parker J. Palmer**, author of *On the Brink of Everything*, *The Courage to Teach*, and *Let Your Life Speak*

"*The Mindful Grandparent* is essential reading for longtime grandparents, grandparents-to-be, and anyone else who seeks to give loving, grandparent-style caring to our young. Marilyn McEntyre and Shirley Showalter show us how grandparenting is both an art and a contemplative practice. They offer a roadmap for navigating the many roles grandparents play, as well as the new and diverse challenges facing their grandchildren."

—**Judith Valente**, former PBS faith and values correspondent and author of *The Art of Pausing* and *How to Be*

"This beautifully written book is filled with love but devoid of sentimentality—richly affirming of grandparents while also challenging us to keep growing and learning as we seek to be helpful to today's children and their parents. Here you'll find renewal, inspiration, and genuine help as you respond to a beloved and important calling."

—**Dorothy C. Bass**, author of *Stepmother: Redeeming a Disdained Vocation* and *Receiving the Day: Christian Practices for Opening the Gift of Time*

"This is a book of wisdom, lightly worn, joyfully shared. The scope is generous and fearless, from crafts and games to racism and death. As a pediatrician, I affirm the authors' respectful understanding of children (and parents) and how they flourish. As a grandmother, I treasure what this graceful work teaches me."

—**Margaret Mohrmann**, professor emerita of pediatrics and religious studies at University of Virginia and author of *Attending Children*

"*The Mindful Grandparent* is a warm and delightful invitation to enjoy grandparenting—and to do it well. Chock full of stories, ideas, wisdom, and encouragement, this is a book to keep handy and return to often."

—**Dora Dueck**, award-winning author and grandmother of nine

"Whether you are already a seasoned grandparent or on the threshold of this chapter of your life, this book will challenge you to awaken to who you are in this moment, and who you can become—which, as the authors say, is 'what grandparenting, and life itself, is all about.'"

—**Marlena Fiol**, professor emerita at University of Colorado and author of *Nothing Bad Between Us* and *CALLED*

"This amazing book offers words for every birth-grandparent, step-grandparent, and foster-grandparent. No one who reads this book—a guide filled with practical ideas for caregiving and the hope that mindful grandparenting will change three generations and the world—will ever forget the helpful lists, impressive resources, wise advice, and tender stories that move from page to heart. The authors teach us to 'raise future grandparents.'"

—**Maren C. Tirabassi**, pastor and author of twenty-two books

"*The Mindful Grandparent* offers a wealth of stories, suggestions, and ideas for grandparents, blending Marilyn McEntyre and Shirley Showalter's personal experiences and thoughtful reflections with solid but unobtrusive research. With these two canny, good-humored, knowledgeable guides, among a host of fellow travelers like Maria Montessori, Walt Whitman, and Mary Oliver, both new and experienced grandparents—and anyone seeking fresh ways of relating to children—will find much here to treasure and to practice."

—**Jeff Gundy**, distinguished poet-in-residence, Bluffton University, and author of *Wind Farm: Landscape with Stories and Towers* and other books

THE MINDFUL GRANDPARENT

THE MINDFUL GRAND- PARENT

The Art of Loving Our Children's Children

Marilyn McEntyre and Shirley Showalter

Broadleaf Books
Minneapolis

THE MINDFUL GRANDPARENT
The Art of Loving Our Children's Children

Cover design: 1517 Media

Print ISBN: 978-1-5064-6806-8
eBook ISBN: 978-1-5064-6807-5

Printed in Canada

*To the grandchildren who have given me so many
reasons to rejoice—Stephen, Matthew, Tommy, Chris,
Benjamin, Hannah, Soren, Ella, and Skye—and
to their remarkable parents, with much love.*

—Marilyn

*And to Owen, Julia, and Lydia: you light up my life.
Anthony and Chelsea, Kate and Nik:
thank you for trusting us with your most precious ones.*

—Shirley

CONTENTS

PART III
FEELINGS

PART IV
GRANDPARENTING BY HAND

PART V
THEIR FUTURE AND OURS

INTRODUCTION

Be astonished.
Tell about it.

—Mary Oliver, "Sometimes"

What good are grandparents at a time like this? It may sound like a dismissive question put that way, but it's a good one to try to answer. What good do we hope to do? What particular gifts do we bring into our children's lives and their children's? How are we to understand grandparenting as a calling? And how, we wondered as we imagined writing this book, might we share what we are learning about that calling with others who are entering into this rewarding, challenging, sometimes bewildering chapter of their own stories?

In the course of many conversations that gave birth to this book, we found out a lot about each other's grandparenting. Shirley bakes more cookies than Marilyn. Marilyn has interred a deceased pill bug by her lemon tree. Shirley knows what to do with oatmeal boxes, fabric scraps, and aging wooden implements. Marilyn has a repertoire of riddles. What Shirley knows about grandparenting began in a Mennonite childhood on a Pennsylvania farm. What Marilyn knows about grandparenting grew out of listening to her own live-in grandparents at a small dinner table in a Southern California suburb.

Both of us continue to enjoy the reading, reflection, conversation, and companionable marriages that have sustained and supported our careers in education. Both of us pay close attention to public life, acutely aware of the immense challenges our grandchildren and their generation already face in disrupted schools, disturbing images on screens, deepening income inequality, and climate change. Both of us are aware, too, of how critical it is to help our white grandchildren humbly participate in the long-overdue reckoning with racism. Both of us pray for those children, their parents, and the many children who are at far greater risk than those we hold close in our family circles.

Social science research can help us take a long view of the calling to the role of grandparent. Anthropologist Kristen Hawkes is credited with the "grandmother hypothesis," which explains evolutionary advancement by the caregiving of two generations and multiple carers rather than only one. Females of many species in the animal world die soon after giving birth to their last offspring. Humans, however, developed extended caregiving roles that linked the elderly to the young. This created a kind of symbiosis in which a long childhood allows extended learning and the wisdom gathered can be passed on to future generations.

Psychology researcher Alison Gopnik, writing in her article "Vulnerable yet Vital" in *Aeon* magazine, concludes that "childhood and old age—those vulnerable, unproductive periods of our lives—turn out, biologically, to be the key to many of our most valuable, deeply human, capacities." If this is true, then grandparents need to do all they can to develop the skills that most aid in building relationships with the young. Patience and storytelling are two of the most cherished values of older age. One could name many more, but all of them lead to that sacred place of connection where love flourishes and learning grows.

That connection happens in the course of many learning moments. *Moments* is a key word: these chapters don't provide a chronological, step-by-step guide to grandparenting. They are by no means comprehensive. This isn't a "study" or an overview; though our professional lives have been spent in academic settings, this is not an academic book. Rather, we like to think of it as an invitation to other grandparents to reflect on their own moments of learning, growth, amusement, concern, and altered awareness.

As we find our way into the lives of little people who need us in ways no one imagines at the outset, we are changed. The passage from parent to grandparent differs from all other changes in our lives because it involves not only a new dimension of our identity but also a transformative shift in relationship with the adult children we love. It is a delicate transition: we step in, we step back; we witness, we help where we can, we make room for new needs and life-changing surprises.

"Mindful grandparenting" is what we've chosen to call this effort to bring attention and care and love to our children's children. Jon Kabat-Zinn in *Full Catastrophe Living* has named seven attitudes of mindfulness: nonjudging, patience, beginner's mind, trust, nonstriving, acceptance, and letting go. These approaches apply to all of life and are especially relevant at the point of change—what we might think of as the threshold time, or liminal space. Theologian

Richard Rohr has called the threshold experience "God's waiting room." Grandparents find themselves in God's waiting room often.

As we wrote these chapters, we encouraged each other to be mindful of our own memories, observations, conversations with other grandparents, and, in some instances, research. The stories we tell about our own grandchildren are ones that have helped us understand children and ourselves in new ways. The resources we offer at the end of each chapter have been helpful to us as well—they are not comprehensive but are representative of the wealth of material available. We hope these resources enrich what we can offer—and receive—as active, engaged, open-hearted elders.

Elder is a term to reclaim. It's one thing to hear it in a marketing context: ads for residential facilities that provide "elder care," for instance. It's another to hear it in a legal or political context—in warnings about "elder abuse" or observations about "elders" (or "seniors") as a voting bloc. Some of us hear it in church contexts as a title for those ordained to particular ministries. But when we think of reclaiming the term and of applying it to ourselves, we think about how it is understood in Indigenous communities. According to Dr. Beatrice Medicine in *Learning to Be an Anthropologist and Remaining "Native,"* in those communities, elders are seen as "repositories of cultural and philosophical knowledge and are the transmitters of such information."

Not all old people are elders in this sense; it's a term that entails both earned authority and responsibility to the community. If we aspire to claim our authority and carry it graciously, and to be of service to younger people, we have a lot of listening to do.

The terms of both public and private life have changed profoundly in ways Alvin Toffler began to articulate in *Future Shock*. Published in 1970, that book focused on the accelerating pace of change and what it would take to adapt as quickly as we have had to in the decades since then. When Marilyn's daughter, then in high school, gently said, "Mom, it's not the way it was when you were in school," Marilyn realized how much she needed to learn. Pocketing lunch money and bus passes, her daughter and her peers walked into a rather more complicated social, institutional, electronic, and political environment every morning than we elders did at their ages. Digital devices, a wider and wilder range of TV programming, highly politicized education and health care policies, anxieties about gun violence: all these things have changed the way they live and move and socialize and the degree of supervision they've come to tolerate and expect. We were not so closely watched nor so assailed by constant choices. As parents and grandparents, we'd do well to observe, and listen, and consider the manifold ways the world has changed.

That said, we can claim and even celebrate those generational differences. If we have homes with slightly slower rhythms—if we lead quieter lives than our adult children, who face demands that have diminished for us—we may be able to offer refuge, respite, or periodic reframing of what our grandchildren have come to think of as "normal." We can provide perspective and, if we live nearby, perhaps a pause in the week. We might be able to afford the time to linger over small things and remind our grandchildren, and ourselves, that the small things are actually big things in disguise.

Or maybe, if we're still working, we can model aging in a way that teaches the children that adults' lives are rich and varied and interesting even after they become grandparents. We are grandparents, yes; but grandparenting may be only one part of life stories that are worth hearing.

We hope that our reflections may be useful to you, our readers, and also that this book might encourage you and other grandparents, especially those who live in very different circumstances than we do, to share your own learning moments. None of us has to invent this wheel. While we come into parenting and grandparenting with more or less examined notions of how to do it, the happy task of grandparenting takes us to a new learning edge. Maybe we can meet one another there.

PART I

THE

WIDENING

CIRCLE

When I was one
I had just begun . . .

—A. A. Milne

WHAT TO EXPECT WHEN THEY'RE EXPECTING

Shirley

Pretty joy!
Sweet joy, but two days old.
Sweet Joy I call thee:
Thou dost smile,
I sing the while;
Sweet joy befall thee!

　　　　　—William Blake, "Infant Joy"

I received the news that I would become a grandmother on the phone. My son and daughter-in-law shared their secret and asked us to hold it with them.

A few short weeks later, they called again. "We lost the baby," my son choked out, but then he moved on to say, in his usually steady voice, that they would try again. A few months later, the same thing happened: phone call one, then phone call two.

I worried. I knew that pregnancy losses put stress on a marriage. Would the newlywed but adult children (ages thirty-five and thirty-seven) get discouraged? If they couldn't have children, would they lose the bloom of their love?

I wasn't thinking about the fact that I might never become a grandparent. I was still busy with my career, not knitting baby blankets in hopeful anticipation.

When the third good-news call came from Anthony and Chelsea, we steeled ourselves for another loss. Two months passed. Then three. We started to get hopeful since none of the miscarriages had progressed this far. We asked our Catholic friends to light candles, and we lit them ourselves in every cathedral we visited. Our prayers were mostly silent, our thoughts constant.

Month four passed. Then five. Every month we relaxed a little more until, at last, the baby reached full term.

Then came the call from Brooklyn: "We're headed to St. Luke's Hospital!" For the next few hours, we did not need Saint Paul to tell us to pray without ceasing. A week later, we held Owen William Showalter in our arms and entered a new world.

Safe arrival had been our first concern. Now we could give ourselves fully to loving Owen, relearning how to hold and diaper and soothe and burp a baby. It wasn't as easy as riding a bike!

When Owen was nine months old, his parents tried for another baby. This time, we were present to hear the news.

This time, there were no sad follow-up calls. Julia Jane burst upon the scene after a normal pregnancy, and we were in the apartment with Owen, taking him to St. Luke's to greet his sister just a few hours after her birth.

We thought perhaps Owen and Julia would be our only grandchildren. Our daughter Kate had told us not to make any assumptions. So when Kate and Nik called from Pittsburgh, seven years after Anthony and Chelsea had, to announce that they were expecting a baby, I was truly surprised—and delighted. By that time, Stuart and I were quite experienced grandparents and were eager to welcome another child into our daughter's family and into our larger family.

Now Lydia, our third grandchild, is three years old. This year, all our children and grandchildren will converge at our home in the Shenandoah Valley of Virginia. Owen, Julia, and Lydia will continue to build "cousin world," a project they started when they first met each other. They convene in the basement, where we store vintage toys and books (their parents' leftovers), on the deck, where we drink mocha (one drop of coffee in a half cup of hot chocolate), and in the driveway, where they fly down the hill on little cars we got at a garage sale.

Advent and Christmas always bring back the memories of those five phone calls, announcing pregnancies. Is it sacrilege to think of human birth news as an annunciation, not unlike that of Mary, the mother of Jesus? Is it strange to imagine they deserve a response like Mary's song in what we know as the Magnificat? I like to think it is just the opposite.

As a mother, I know a tiny iota of Mary's awe and joy, but the fraction I know deepens my desire to know the Creator God who entered into the world the same way you and I did.

As a grandmother, I wonder about Mary's mother, wishing the nativity scene included her.

The Christmas carols I have sung joyfully all my life have always moved me. But one, especially, has changed for me since I became a grandma. It's often the last song in the Christmas Eve service, sung as we pass the flame down the row to light each other's candles. As soon as I sing "all is calm, all is bright," I think of hearing the phone ring. This year, I might light my candle from the candle of one of my precious three grandchildren, each one a miracle, each one a reflection of God's great love. Together, we will sing, "Silent night, holy night / All is calm, all is bright / 'Round yon virgin / Mother and Child / Holy infant so tender and mild / Sleep in heavenly peace / Sleep in heavenly peace."

Suggestions for Grandparents

1. Conversations about whether and when to have babies can be hard for couples to manage. It's likely better not to bring up this subject at all. When or if your children choose to talk about their choices or hopes, be as supportive as possible.
2. If miscarriage has been part of your family's journey, there are supportive online communities in both the United States and the United Kingdom. Healingafterpregnancy loss.com and miscarriageassociation.org.uk may prove useful places to do research and find community.
3. Holidays such as Christmas, Hanukkah, and Kwanzaa offer many opportunities to strengthen the ties of family love and to be reminded that these ties are sacred. Attending services together is just the beginning.

2

LABORS OF LOVE

Marilyn

This first-time grandma was her daughter's rock.
—Caroline Bologna, comment
in a birth room photo essay

I didn't take for granted that any of my daughters would want me to be in the birthing room when their babies were born. I had never thought about inviting my own mother, since we were living at the time on the other side of the world. I'm not sure I would have, as much as I loved her—so I was surprised and touched each time the invitation from my daughters came. From one it was to accompany her through labor and then to let her and her husband have the room to themselves in those shocking, sacred minutes immediately preceding and following delivery. From two others, it was to be there the entire time, coaching, breathing with them, softly and repeatedly reminding them to let their strong bodies do what they were designed to do.

All their husbands were there, too, engaged in their different ways, willing if not eager to see their beautiful wives in pain they really couldn't do much about. All of them had read the requisite books—*What to Expect When You're Expecting*, *Mindful Birthing*, *The Thinking Woman's Guide to a Better Birth*, or their equivalents. I had read a few of my own over the years and had cause to be grateful not only for the abundant guidance available but also for the legacy of a missionary mother who had attended many births and deaths with capable, cheerful, kindly, quiet encouragement.

I remembered my own labor, of course, each time. I remembered learning to negotiate with my body about how to meet each contraction with breath and intention. I remembered the power of repetition: "Shallow breaths." "You can completely relax now until the next one comes." "Your body knows what to do." "I'm right here." I remembered the radical amazement when the head crowned and a tiny being emerged from my body as if this particular miracle had never happened before—and it hadn't.

It was helpful to know ahead of time exactly what each daughter wanted from me and to have made sure that each son-in-law was comfortable with the decision to have me in the room. It was a happy task to arrange ritual objects where they could provide the grounding and beauty each daughter needed. It was exhilarating to be so deeply focused on one thing with such fierce, loving attention for all the hours it took—eighteen in one case—and to feel my own energies synchronizing with each beautiful woman I had brought into the world. It was humbling to watch each daughter find something heroically strong and resilient in herself and bring it forth. It was scary to know that things could go wrong. (Things do: one baby was taken to the NICU for extra oxygen and stayed there for his first three days.) It was awesome in the best and richest sense of that overused word to feel that we were stepping into a long, ancient lineage of women who had helped women bring new life into the world. It's good that fathers are now so routinely invited to be part of the process. Yet there is still a dimension of childbirth that is a female ritual, mysterious even to us but belonging to us as a birthright.

I learned the dance a little differently each time—when to lean in, when to rub her head or back, when to step away and let her husband take the lead, when to speak, when to be silent. I learned to let tears come when they surfaced, almost an unnoticed, accepted, and undramatic part of my own body's complete consent to the demands of the moment.

One labor went somewhat awry: the baby wouldn't rotate into position and remained transverse for hours. Finally, after what seemed to me an unseemly delay, his mama was whisked off to the operating room for a last-minute cesarean delivery. Only the father was allowed in with her. Standing nearby in the hallway, I heard a cry come from her that shook my whole body as (I later learned) they reached in to try one last time to move the baby into place. I wouldn't have thought her capable of a sound like that. When that baby emerged in his dad's arms, bundled and breathing softly, no one would have guessed what a production his appearance had required. I laughed at how utterly untroubled he seemed to be—as though drowsily wondering what the fuss was all about.

Those first hours and days were full of other family folk waiting in the hospital hallways, sharing snacks, speculating, asking for updates every time I took a bathroom break. I was honored to be the sweaty messenger and, finally, to step back and enjoy their delighted cooing over the tiny toes and waving hands when their turn came. Relinquishing the little person, now a part of the rest of my own life, to parents, other grandparents, eager aunties, and other fond people in the wide circles of love in my daughters' lives was the first step into a role that keeps unfolding.

It's still a dance: come in close, step back and let others in, wait for invitation, honor their intimate space, speak when they ask or when the Spirit guides you, learn to hold your peace. And when a new thing happens—another baby, an illness, a move, a career change—be ready to stand by and remind them: "Breathe." "Relax into this." "Call on the deep part of you that knows what to do." "Allow." "Surrender." "Say yes."

Suggestions for Grandparents

1. If you're invited to be present for any part of a baby's arrival, books might help you imagine your own role, understand your own hopes and limits, and take stock of your own anxieties. Penny Simkin's *The Birth Partner* and *The Art of Coaching for Childbirth* by Neri Life Choma and Christine Morton are good places to start.

2. It's good to have as specific a conversation as possible ahead of time so that you don't overstep and so that you

step up at the right time. Those hours are tender and also touchy. She may change her mind midstream about what she needs—even about wanting you there. It's good to gird your loins, know not to take offense, remember that she's in charge, and call on your own spiritual resources to practice flexibility, openness to the call of the moment, and deep, prayerful gratitude for what love calls forth in each of us.

YOUR NEW NAME

Shirley

A good name is better than precious ointment.
—Ecclesiastes 7:1

"What do you want to be called?" is the first question friends and family ask when they know you will be a grandparent soon.

It wasn't always this way. Fifty years ago, grandparent names, like Neapolitan ice cream, came in three flavors. Most formal was "Grandmother and Grandfather." Most common was "Grandma and Grandpa." Least formal was "Grandmom and Grandpop." Sometimes the names were shortened to "Grammy and Gramps."

Today, however, names for grandparents exceed even the expanded menu for ice cream. Just a quick survey among my friends—What do your grandchildren call you?—yielded this variety for grandmothers: Bubbe, Grammie, Gram, Oma, Aama, Poppi, Nana, Bani, Ga, Mommom, Meemaw, Bapi, Mormor. And for grandfathers: Zayde, Poppo, Papa, Jum, Opa, Pa, Bumpum, Gepaw, Papaw, Peepaw.

Grandparent names are a wonderful opportunity to connect children to their family history and cultural heritage. Sometimes other languages offer good choices: Oma and Opa. Also, Poppi, Poppo, mentioned earlier, came from this source. We could add Abuelita, Tito, Bibi, Tatu, Nyanya, Nkuku, Ugogo, Babu, Ntatemogolo, and Ubabamkhulu. Yanick Rice Lamb wrote an essay, "The 'G' Word: Grandmas Who Don't Want to Be Called Grandma," for BlackAmericaWeb.com explaining why she wants to be called "Nini" and why many Black grandmothers prefer to make up new names or revive African names.

Sometimes the name stays fluid until the child tries to say it—hence one-syllable names like Ga and Pa. Even if the child chooses the name, the grandparent chooses whether to accept it.

Maybe you'll want Goldie Hawn's name: "Glamma." Or try these on for size: Bubba, Sonoma, and Napa. If you like these, be prepared to have people compare them to franchised restaurants, Apple's latest operating system, or Subaru models.

Grandparent names have become so variable that my niece and her husband like to tease their teenagers: "Someday, if you have kids, they must call us 'Bobbie' and 'Captain.'" According to my niece, this proclamation has evoked the desired effect: groaning and eye-rolling.

Of course, you could just go by your version of "Shirley" and "Stu." Five percent of grandparents choose to have their grandchildren call them by their given names.

Looking at all these options, you might not guess that "Grandma" and "Grandpa" still remain the most popular choices in the United States. One study suggests that 70 percent of grandmothers and 60 percent of grandfathers are referred to by some form of "Grandma" and "Grandpa."

The name you eventually choose can be a signal about the kind of relationship you seek with your grandchild as well as the way you envision yourself. Is your self-image that of a young person or an older person, for example? (According to one study, the actual age of grandparents varies between about thirty-eight and one hundred, and the average age is fifty.) The more informal the name, the younger it might sound. The more unusual, the more it can lead to the question, "What's the story behind your name?"

I picked my grandparent name in 2011: "Grandma." I hadn't heard most of the aforementioned names (the variety has definitely increased in the last decade). But even if I had looked more carefully at other options, I think I would still prefer a simple "Grandma." I lost my Grandma Hess when I was three years old and so have only the memories my mother has given me: "She had a great personality. Her customers at the Central Market loved her. And she was so happy that her only daughter had a daughter."

On the other side of the family was my Grandma Hershey, a kind, patient, loving woman of ample bosom and skillful hands. She made afghans for grandchildren and comforters at the sewing circle. She *was* a comforter.

So Grandma I became. I am probably more like Grandma Hess than I am like Grandma Hershey. Grandma Hess's Central Market was better entertainment than a carnival to me, and I have loved connecting to others in public ways as she did. Yet now I get to expand my ability to be a quiet presence, like Grandma Hershey was. No fanfare. No sewing either. My version of calm is listening, reading books, playing, and making soft-boiled eggs in her memory.

Owen and Julia have two grandmas. They keep us straight by calling us "Grandma Nancy" and "Grandma Shirley," along with "Granddad Clayton" and "Granddad Stuart." Lydia has a Grammie and a Grandma to go with Pops and Granddad. All of us are happy with these choices. Marilyn and her husband have two sets of names: Amma and Appa for four grandchildren and Grandma and Grandpa Mac for the other five.

But a rose by any other name would smell as sweet.

Suggestions for Grandparents

1. Naming is a sacred act. My favorite book about naming is Madeleine L'Engle's *A Wind in the Door*, part of the trilogy that begins with *A Wrinkle in Time*. This is a wonderful series to read to children after about age eight. When L'Engle signed my son's copy of this book, she wrote, "Be a Namer!"

2. If you want more name choices, there's a book for you: *The New Grandparents Name Book: A Lighthearted Guide to Picking the Perfect Grandparent Name* (ArtStone Press). Written by the mother-and-daughter team Lin Wellford and Skye Pifer, it offers seven hundred creative options.

3. Unless you are sure you want a particular name, you might want to wait before you decide. The process of making choices and including multiple generations always has the potential to help you understand what is important to others. It is also a good opportunity to tell children about the kind of grandparent you admire and want to become.

4. The statistics in this chapter can be found in the 2018 AARP study of grandparents (you can find it at aarp.org). Since AARP has been studying grandparents for a long time, you might find it a good source for many questions.

5. The internet provides a number of funny videos on the topic, including "Choosing a Grandmother Name Is Serious Business." Type that phrase into your browser and enjoy!

A MOTHER'S BLESSING

Shirley

For it was you who formed my inward parts;
you knit me together in my mother's womb.
                                    —Psalm 139:13

When Lydia was waiting to be born, growing more active every day in her mother's womb, my daughter's friends concocted a brilliant scheme. They invited about twenty young women and me to gather for a Mother's Blessing.

Kate and I traveled to the center of Pittsburgh and took the elevator up to the top of a beautifully restored Frick Building, which was, at the time, a working space for women artists and entrepreneurs. As we passed through the elegant double doors, our senses went into overdrive. Down the middle of the room stretched a table full of tropical fruits, cheeses, shrimp cocktail, and other succulent tidbits. Wineglasses lined the wall to the right. Each woman brought a favorite dish, a blessing, and a bead (to make a special necklace). After enjoying delectable food and drink, we sat in a circle. Kate was given a floral crown and seated next to a white organdy tepee draped over wooden poles, a nod to the Indigenous tradition for which the Mother's Blessing is named.

Each friend spoke about some experience she had with Kate or shared her own mothering advice. I recognized in the stories the essence of my daughter, so creative and kind. Kate began to glow from the inside out. Looking at her face, I saw the baby who had taken only two hours to travel the length of the birth canal, the little girl who sprinted up the stairs to find her kitty, and the young art major searching for ways to find and make beauty.

As the storytelling continued, we laughed and cried and shared hopes, fears, and silly motherhood missteps. Someone read "A Mother's Prayer for Her Daughter" by Tina Fey, making everyone laugh.

My contribution was to bring some antique items that stretched more than one hundred years: from my great-grandmother's hand-crocheted doily to the little heart-shaped turquoise stone I had recently purchased in Santa Fe. I also shared a psalm with the group: "For you formed my inward parts; you knit me together in my mother's womb." I have pressed this verse into the hands of numerous parents-and grandparents-to-be over the years. But this time was different. This time my baby was having a baby.

This time she was joining a long line of mothers going back beyond both of us and ending with a Divine Mother. I imagined a Mothering God standing as a shepherdess among the sheep, knitting wool into souls and knitting all souls into a shawl that encircles the whole world. I prayed a blessing upon my daughter and upon her daughter still being knit. I added my bead to all the others.

Today a lovely, large necklace hangs on a jewelry board made by Lydia's daddy and stored in Kate's closet. When Kate is ready for Lydia to know the story of the necklace, she will take it down and place it in Lydia's hands so that she can hold it, hear about how her mommy and daddy loved her even before she was born, and then return the necklace to its special place.

After Lydia has been introduced to the Mother's Blessing necklace, I plan to invite her to find the little turquoise heart bead I placed there. I will tell her stories about all the friends and mothers and grandmothers who helped knit her together while she was still in her mommy's belly.

"Do you think we can love someone even before we can see them?" I will ask.

Suggestions for Grandparents

1. Many variations of blessings, baby showers, and other prebirth rituals exist. You can create your own, keeping in mind not only the many needs of a new nursery but also the needs of the family and friend community to bless and celebrate. Ideas for planning a Mother's Blessing can be found by searching online. Whatever you do before birth can become part of a new grandchild's "origin story."

2. You might want to plant a tree for the new baby at your house or the baby's house.

3. If the idea of a Mothering God becomes an important part of your journey to grandparenthood, you will find inspiration in Bobby McFerrin's "The 23rd Psalm" on any music streaming service and on the album *Medicine Music* (1990). A book such as *The Feminine Face of God: The Unfolding of the Sacred in Women* by Sherry Ruth Anderson and Patricia Hopkins might enlarge your vision and offer deeper connections between the birthing process and larger spiritual and cultural traditions.

5

WELCOME TO THE WORLD, BABY GIRL

Marilyn

The child is both a hope and a promise.
—Maria Montessori

Our sweet young neighbors had just brought their brand-new daughter home from the hospital. We made a big sign to greet her that said, "Welcome to the World, Baby Girl!" It was meant to be a celebratory gesture. We were social distancing in those months of pandemic lockdown, so we couldn't hold that baby or hug her parents. That constraint made me wistful as I lettered the sign. Inking in the big exclamation point, a creeping sense of irony was unavoidable: What kind of world were we welcoming her into? Right now, for her, and for her big sister, who is just learning to ride a bike without training wheels, this world is still "vast and beautiful and new." Her parents are kind, her neighbors delight in her, her oversized labradoodle, Luna, trots alongside her on their excursions around the block, offering her vaguely benevolent protection.

Of course, we want to protect them too—our neighbors' children, our children's children, all the little ones coming into a world afflicted by pandemic and police violence and political rancor and unstable systems. I wonder, though, how long "protection" that keeps them blissfully unaware can or should last. Even five-year-olds, if they're in school, have lately been subject to lockdown drills in the wake of school shootings. Racial epithets and verbal hostilities add static to their soundscapes before they can fully register what they mean. Many children, especially children of color, learn wariness shockingly early. They have to.

One of our grandchildren showed signs of anxiety very early—before the age of three. He is older now and more able to do a reasonable risk assessment. But I imagine he will wrestle with recurrent anxieties for a long time. His experience, in particular, makes me wonder how to find a balance between "protecting" the innocence of the very young and "preparing" them.

Perhaps addressing the tricky matter of educating children should begin with an audit of our own concerns. What do we think we need protection from? When does prudence become insularity? Where are those of us who are white prone to unconscious or uncritical acceptance of policing that offers "safety" selectively and at a high cost to those who are far more likely than white people to be targeted, apprehended, and incarcerated? How can we teach even small children the kind of courage it takes to recognize injustice and stand against bullies?

Several recent articles suggest that the problem of bullying has escalated over the past few years, even among small children. (A few of these are listed in the "Suggestions for Grandparents" section.) It may start wherever two or three are gathered together: on the rug, for example, with toys to be grabbed. And it may be that we can help curb those very early violent impulses more effectively if we see them through the wide-angle lens of cultural training. That rug is where we begin to teach justice—not just as a moral or religious principle but as a practice that fosters community. Even very small children flourish, Maria Montessori taught, when they are given an actual participatory role in maintaining the health of the family or community. For instance, a very little one, if she can walk, can be deputized to close the door or carry napkins to the table or distribute drawing paper. And even that very little one may be taught that everyone does better when everyone does better. Interestingly, Montessori also discourages rewarding or overpraising. Such responses from adults can detract from the simple satisfaction a child may take in doing her part, not because it's cute or because she can bask in adult approval but because she has a real role in something bigger than herself.

This may seem idealistic, but I've seen it work. The little girl next door sleeping near her big, curly haired dog has work ahead of her. It's work that we and her parents and her generation will need her to do. We are her trainers. It's our job, sooner rather than later, to help her connect the dots that lead her out of her playroom and into the park—so that later, perhaps, if she's led to a protest march, she'll know what to do and why she's there.

Suggestions for Grandparents

1. It's helpful to read up on bullying if only not to be naive about the social complexities that begin for many in the earliest months of social exposure. Some helpful articles can be found here:
https://www.stopbullying.gov/resources/facts
https://www.naeyc.org/resources/blog/bullying-early -childhood
https://www.broadbandsearch.net/blog/cyber-bullying -statistics
A couple of books (among a variety of good ones) for early training and to read to young listeners are *What Should Danny Do?* by Adir and Ganit Levy and *Seeds and Trees* by Brandon Walden.

2. As children become old enough to have conversations about their feelings, one way to widen the frame on behavioral choices is to play a "What do you think will happen?" game: "OK, if you take the truck away from Joey, what do you think will happen?" "If Joey keeps the truck for five more minutes, what do you think will happen?" Helping children follow the ripples outward from an action in an imaginative, playful way can give them valuable training in tracing consequences.

6

COULD YOU, SHOULD YOU BE A GRANDNANNY?

Shirley

The people I love the best
jump into work head first.

    —Marge Piercy, "To Be of Use"

I first heard of the "grandnanny" concept when friends accepted the invitation of their son and daughter-in-law to move to Boston for a year after the birth of their grandbabies. The grandparent couple took the place of a nanny, got to enjoy the benefits of living in and exploring a lovely city, and saved the parents both money and anxiety by providing loving, in-home care.

Talk about a win-win-win! When they returned to our small city in the Shenandoah Valley, our friends gushed about their exciting year. My husband, Stuart, and I tucked the grandnanny story away in case we might want to imitate it someday.

As it turned out, I became a grandmother at an opportune time. If it had happened a year earlier, I would have been working full-time. But in 2011, my years of obligation to paid employment had ended. Stuart was still working, but his hours were flexible and part-time.

Our son and daughter-in-law lived in Brooklyn, New York, in a high-rise above the Brooklyn Academy of Music. Would they welcome us as grandnannies? We decided to ask. When they were expecting, we told them our friends' story and asked what they thought about the idea.

My daughter-in-law, a very careful planner and organizer, had questions. We were just getting to know each other, since she and our son had been married only two years when Owen was born. Our son naturally gravitates to strategy and finance, so he investigated apartments within walking distance of their condo. There was a small but beautiful one in a new high-rise six blocks away. It turned out that renting an apartment was less expensive than hiring a full-time nanny. The idea was getting more and more attractive.

"Could you learn baby CPR?" asked our daughter-in-law. We investigated our local options. Sure enough, the Red Cross provided a child and baby CPR class. We signed up, got certified, and carry baby CPR instruction cards in our wallets to this day.

Once we showed our commitment and the logistics were settled, the invitation to go to Brooklyn grew firm. We picked a moving date, advertised our own home as a furnished apartment for grad students at the local university, and waited for all the details to fall into place. They did!

For ten months, we lived on the twelfth floor of the Toren building and walked each day to the twenty-third floor of the Forté. In addition to this round-trip trek, we often wheeled Owen to a nearby shopping mall or to Fort Greene Park. Stuart and I each took four- to five-hour shifts. One would be there in the morning for the hand-off when Daddy and Mommy went to work. The other would come in time for lunch.

At lunch, the stories of the morning served as the main course, often producing laughter. As Owen got older, he joined us at the table, and we got to see him begin to inspect and ingest "real" food, like broccoli trees and mashed potatoes. The guard would change, and the other adult would put Owen down for a nap and stay until a parent returned.

On our hours off, Stuart was able to do his work, and I drafted most of a book manuscript. Owen enjoyed consistent nurture and lots of adventures. After hours and on weekends, we hit the streets. We memorized the subway paths to some of our favorite haunts: Chinatown, Little Italy, and Times Square. Brooklyn Heights and DUMBO (Down Under Manhattan Bridge Overpass) were just ten or fifteen blocks away. We walked. And walked. Like real New Yorkers.

The year flew by, and we returned to the Shenandoah Valley with many happy memories and a skin-to-skin bond with Owen that goes deeper than the epidermis. We returned to Brooklyn after Owen's sister, Julia, was born, five months after we left. This time our schedule was too full to offer a move to Brooklyn—and, frankly, we weren't sure we could handle two children under the age of two! Their parents found excellent childcare.

So six years later, when we got the news that our daughter and son-in-law were expecting a baby, we looked at our schedules and wondered if we could make the grandnanny offer again. We offered, and they said yes. Kate and Nik had the benefit of observing our first grandnanny gig, in which we all emerged unscathed.

Kate and Nik lived in Pittsburgh. They are millennials, creatively piecing together various entrepreneurial enterprises. At the time they were expecting Lydia, their gigs included being a freelance software developer, apartment managers, and Airbnb super hosts. Oh yes, and they were renovating a one-hundred-year-old house that had gone into foreclosure and had not been lived in for years. Downed trees littered the backyard, and only the bones of the brick house were salvageable.

Did we want to jump into their world? Were we flexible enough to go with the flow of a baby, plumbers, carpenters, and tree-trimmers? We hoped so. By the time Lydia was three months old, we were on the road with our computers and clothes loaded into the back seat, ready to try to be helpful.

During the ten months we lived in Pittsburgh, we moved apartments four times and spent one week living with Kate, Nik, and the baby in the one-bedroom apartment they rented as a placeholder while the contractors were sanding floors and wood trim in the house down the hill. Kate and Nik made pillows and a sofa into a living room "nest," eking out enough sleep to survive, while Stuart and I got the bed.

Lydia rolled with all the changes and hit all her milestones on time. In the midst of the chaos, she kept us focused on the most important thing: her health and well-being.

By October, we had a lovely small apartment carved out of what had been the attic of their old house. We moved into it, enjoying the sunrise view of the hilly city through the tall steeples of an old church and the evening sunlight reflected in the windows of the houses across the street.

We sent Nik, Kate, and Lydia off to the other grandparents for Thanksgiving. Hoping to put gratitude into action and to surprise them while they ate turkey two hundred miles away, we found paint, brushes, old sheets, and buckets. We tackled the wooden railing around the new porch, laying on first primer and then another coat of white paint. The work proceeded more slowly than we had hoped, but we had music and podcasts and occasional chats with neighbors to make the time go faster. As we neared the end of the project, hours before the family was scheduled to appear, we congratulated ourselves. We went to Target and bought a welcome mat as the pièce de résistance. We were rewarded by a tearful daughter, a grateful son-in-law, and a bouncy baby girl when they returned.

By Christmas, the house was 90 percent finished and ready to be the base for the whole family to celebrate. Anthony, Chelsea, Owen, and Julia traveled to be with us. We found a free Christmas tree on the street and dragged it home, placing it in the perfect spot in the corner of the foyer, just under the stained-glass window, the crown jewel of the house.

In late May, we left Pittsburgh, just as we had left Brooklyn years before, feeling enormously enriched. And as far as we know, no children, grandchildren, or parents were harmed!

Suggestions for Grandparents

1. Are you a candidate for this kind of intensive infant care? Here are a few questions to help you discern:
   - Relationships, communication skills, and shared expectations matter most. Do the parents want you to come? What fears need to be faced? Does it sound like fun or a burden to you?
   - Are you blessed with good health?
   - Is your work flexible?
   - Can you make the finances work? (We live in a university town and have demand for our house as a rental, which helped us afford to go.)
   - Did you get infant CPR training?
2. There are many other models of three-generational childcare if this one does not work for you. If you live close by, you may offer (or may be asked) to do one or two days per week or after school. Or more. Ideally, whatever the childcare agreement, both parents and grandparents are giving and gaining freely and reciprocally. Some people build new spaces that are permanent homes merged together (cohousing) or move into the larger of two houses together.
3. You may be a guardian or custodial grandparent, providing full-time care. Nearly three million grandparents are intensive caregivers! If you are one of them, find as many others to help as possible, and don't sacrifice your own health. There may be special resources in your community, like the one at Georgia State University: Project Healthy Grandparents.

7

NOW WE ARE SIX

Marilyn

Blood makes you related; love makes you family.
—anonymous

We all converged in the hall outside of the newborn nursery: new grandparents, some of us by blood, some by remarriage. All of us were making various cooing sounds as we gazed in astonishment at Stephen, our first grandchild. He had a pretty big team already, this little guy.

More than 50 percent of us live in blended families. Multiple websites cite that number, though it varies somewhat according to what kinds of "blended" families are included. A lot of children are being raised not by parents and stepparents but by grandparents, or by a grandparent and a single parent, or by a grandparent and a much older sibling . . . the list of possibilities goes on.

I had cause to do some research of my own in this area years ago when I married a man with children whose first wife had died. We had six children between us. Neither of us had foreseen that particular plot development in our life stories. Those years of helping our children grow up in new, more complicated circumstances were difficult and full of grace (and may deserve their own telling another time). But part of that story belongs here. Six of our eight grandchildren have six grandparents. In some families, there may be more, depending on remarriages and who gets involved in the grandparenting.

Most grandparents have to—or get to, depending on how you look at it—share grandchildren with at least one, two, or three others who occupy the role. By and large, this is a good thing: extended families, in most places, for most of history, have been the norm. Children get passed around. In some cultures, all close elders are "Grandmother" or "Grandfather." Children develop a wide circle of trust. They have access to a wide range of personal styles and opinions and ways of receiving and expressing love. One grandmother may teach a child to bake bread, another the rudiments of gardening or animal care. One grandfather may take a grandchild with him to church and another to the synagogue. Many grandparents still work, or travel, and show up at intervals of several months bearing souvenirs and stories. Their visits are special occasions when business as usual stops and the weekend becomes a party. Their cograndparents, on the other hand, may live in town, pick the kids up from school a couple of days a week, oversee lessons, attend soccer games, and play a more active part in discipline and decision-making. From a child's point of view, one grandma may be the "fun" one and another one distant but interesting and, as the child gets older, an object of maturing curiosity as conversations deepen.

I had the great privilege of being present for the birth of six of our grandchildren—unforgettable experiences for which I'm deeply grateful. The day after the first of them came into the world, another grandmother and I arrived together in Elizabeth's hospital room and took turns holding Stephen, both duly amazed and amused by his little nose and fingers and small, squeaky sounds. It was a sweet moment of sharing. It was also a little learning moment; we were all in this together, and always would be. We would all be showing up at performances and graduations and basketball games. We would all be on the hotline when Stephen got sick or injured and on the grapevine when there was a new anecdote to share.

There is, of course, a difficult side to all this togetherness. I remember little flashes of possessiveness, jealousy, competitiveness, and apprehension about time-sharing and love-sharing in this precious little person's life. Those little shadow spots came and went like floaters in the eye. They still come and go. Mostly I'm very grateful on the grandchildren's behalf that they have such a supportive circle of caring adults in their lives.

That circle keeps expanding. It will include teachers, of course, and coaches and "aunties" and "uncles" not related by blood, and friends' parents and grandparents. The assignment—and it's a joyful one—is to find and foster with each of them a tendril of connection that can take root and grow into the strong, mature, trusting relationship I so hope for. Those may begin on the floor where we move blocks around and make stories to go with our structures, maybe continuing one day in an architectural tour of San Francisco, or in reading the same book again and again and later writing one together.

Some of the other grandparents have more money than we do. They'll be the ones, no doubt, to provide more expensive tickets and trips. Some have holiday rituals and schedules our adult children feel it's important to honor, so we'll be working with and around those as we develop our own. All of us are going to have to keep coming to terms with the fact that none of us gets a final vote on holidays or homemaking or discipline or choice of schools. We're the supporting cast.

And that, my grand-folk friends, is very good news. There's freedom in being a witness rather than a primary player. There are parts of child-raising we no longer have the energy for—and we don't have to. If our knees or hips are creaky, we don't have to be the ones on the floor with blocks. If we loathe Barbie dolls, we don't have to play with them. I've simply declared a few of those limits. I get to say, "I'll help you build with your blocks, but I don't want to kick the ball around right now." It's part of defining my role. I'm the grandma who does some things and not others. I'm deeply interested in them and their thoughts and questions. I'm not deeply interested in SpongeBob and don't have to pretend to be. I rarely provide candy, and I time-limit noisy, battery-run toys (presents that emphatically did not come from me!).

There's ample opportunity for self-reflection and even fun in deciding what kind of grandma to be. When there are six (or even more!) grandparents, depending on family reshuffling, there may be more of us than these children are going to feel like coping with at times. There will be times to back off. It's good to have significant portions of our own lives that have nothing to do with grandchildren. Then when it's time to read *The Velveteen Rabbit* again, or to change a diaper, or to turn pots into drums, we'll be ready for those particular pleasures. And when we're needed, we'll show up, glad to be part of a team, glad we've lived long enough to take our place among the elders, and glad to discover in ourselves the wisdom in learning how both to step back and to step up.

Suggestions for Grandparents

1. Depending on all parties' openness, it can be valuable to have a few friendly conversations with the other grandparents about how you understand your shared kids' needs. The more openness and laughter those conversations can create, the better. One grandmother and I meet about every six months for coffee and to check in about various shared kids and grandkids. She and I don't inhabit the same social circles, but our worlds overlap, and it's important to both of us to remain in friendly communication about the children we love—the big ones and the small ones.

2. Where there are tensions or great distance or differing values or outright family conflict, cograndparenting can be very tricky. In those cases, it's especially important to be as clear as possible—first with yourself, then with your adult children—about what you'd most like to participate in, what you're eager to do, what you're willing to do, what you're reluctant to do, and where your boundaries

lie. Robert Frost may have been speaking ironically about good fences making good neighbors, but good boundaries do make for clarity and provide an important stay against confusion.

3. Graciousness requires that we defer when it's another family's turn to host the kids and grandkids for an occasion. It can be a real gift to your kids to be proactive at times and suggest that this year you meet up for a pre-Christmas craft party instead of hosting Christmas dinner. Or maybe you could celebrate an off-beat holiday together to make room for another family's holiday celebrations (Shakespeare's birthday? An ancestor's birthday? An Irish or Mexican or Chinese holiday, depending on where those ancestors come from?).

4. Making a picture book of "People Who Love You" can be a lovely project with children. Adding to it, as teachers and new friends come along, may be a significant way to teach them that the circle of love is elastic and large. Each page might include a list of things to appreciate or enjoy about that person.

LINKING TO A LINEAGE

Shirley

Children's children are a crown to the aged,
and parents are the pride of their children.
—Proverbs 17:6 NIV

Do you remember your grandparents? Your great-grandparents? As we adjust to our new roles as grandparents, we naturally try to recall what we learned from our own. Were they good for stories and snuggling? Or were they sticklers for table manners and clean fingernails? Are they the role models we draw on, or do we need to look elsewhere to find the kind of grandparent we want to become?

After becoming a grandmother, I meditated more on my lineage than I ever did before. I have written about my

Hershey grandparents (see chapter 10). On my mother's side
of the family, disruption occurred when my Grandma Hess
died suddenly on June 25, 1951, at age fifty-five. I was just
three years old, so I don't remember her, but I do remember my mother's deep sadness. She told me many times how
much she missed and admired her mother and how generous her mother would have been to me had she lived.

My Grandpa Hess never remarried and had only one
daughter, my mother. Mother invited her father to join us
every Saturday for dinner: a noon meal big enough to fuel
the weekend (on the farm, we had "dinner" and "supper,"
not "lunch" and "dinner"). Mother would make foods she
knew Grandpa enjoyed: baked or fried chicken, roast beef,
potatoes, garden vegetables, canned fruits from our arch cel-
lar, and almost always homemade pie, cake, or cookies. She
would send extras home with her father, and before he left,
he would tuck two dollars under his plate. Those bills became
welcome additions to the glass jar cash supply in the kitchen
cupboard, which seldom contained more than ten dollars.

Grandpa Hess lived to be almost ninety-five years old. He
drove a 1942 cream-colored Cadillac and was a genial but
not loquacious presence. My mother loved his twinkling eyes
and pointed them out to us as a sign of his quiet humor. In his
later years, he often recited poems. The fragment I remember now seems very edgy for an old Mennonite grandpa: "A
wonderful bird is the pelican / His beak can hold more than
his belly can / And I don't see how the hell it can!"

When our granddaughter Lydia was born, she was automatically enrolled in all the memories of all the grandparents
before her, on both sides. When I interviewed her father's
parents, Neal and Ila, about their grandparent heritage, I

was touched by Neal's devotion to memory. He had very few memories of his paternal grandfather, who had a stroke that left him mute. "I cherish every family story that fleshes him out as human," said Neal.

It may help all of us to remember that the little children entrusted to us today will eventually review their own memories and cache of family stories, hoping to discover moments of presence in their lives that we now have the power to create.

The birth of a baby brings almost instant awakening to a family. Suddenly, the young parents comprehend in a new way the combination of love and fear, pride and anxiety, encouragement and insecurity that likely buffeted their own parents: "My parents and grandparents did this for me! And now I will do this for my child."

When we gaze upon a new baby, we see our parents gazing upon us, and their parents gazing upon them, in a mirror of infinity going back to the earliest ancestors. Perhaps that is why so many of us, having been told by our friends that grandparenthood is wonderful, nevertheless find ourselves surprised by the explosive impact of those early days. As Grammie Ila put it, "I just wasn't ready for the wave of feeling this baby brought into my life. The experience was the most beautiful thing ever—almost stronger than my feelings for my own babies."

The experience of birth enlarges the view we previously held of our parents. We become at least partially conscious of that fact when we see our parents fall in love with the baby who turned our world upside down.

The blood of those ancestors of ours still runs through our veins. We forgive them their trespasses as we ask in advance for forgiveness for ours. And we thank them for making it possible for us to hold a baby that is the baby of our baby.

Suggestions for Grandparents

1. As you select your own philosophy and style of grandparenting, you will likely recall images and stories of your own grandparents. Find pictures of them and write down memories to share with your children and grandchildren. Ancestry.com can be a rich source of data, including photos, military records, and grave locations.
2. You can download blank family trees from the internet and fill them in (older grandchildren often enjoy helping with this task). Or you can purchase a journal. *Grandmother's Journal: Memories and Keepsakes for My Grandchild* is a journal filled with prompts asking about memories and including a family tree.
3. When a new child is born, you might consider buying a baby memory book that features history and gives you a place for the photos and stories you have collected.

9

BUILDING A GRANDPARENT TEAM

Shirley

You can observe a lot just by watching.
—Yogi Berra

When I was a brand-new college president, totally inexperienced in the field of fundraising, a colleague came to my office with a set of notes about twenty people. With a twinkle in his eye and a slightly ironic tone in his voice, he said, "Here are your new best friends."

Fundraising is indeed easier when donors become your friends, but not all presidents are able to connect with donors at a deep, personal level. I was lucky enough to be among the few. I understood that these generous donors were vital to the well-being of the college we all loved, and so I naturally cared about them and their families. I began to trust them enough to share both triumphs and challenges in the life of the college and in my own life. As time went on, they did indeed become close friends. Long after leaving the presidency, I still care about them and feel their concern for me and my family. We all care about the college that brought us together.

Perhaps there is an analogy for grandparents here. Did you look across the aisle at the wedding of your adult child to the new spouse's parents and think, *These are my new best friends?* Your child's decision to marry their child has bonded you to this family. Your fate is tied to theirs in ways you cannot yet predict.

Sometimes the families surrounding a young couple have known each other for years and have already formed what sociologists call "thick" relationships, with multiple points of intersection: possibly neighborhood, school, church, or work. More often, in our mobile age, the relationship between parents of the couple does not exist prior to engagement and marriage. Many couples are taking more time to commit to each other, and with careers often dictating moves to different locations, relationships between families on both sides can take a long time to form.

When grandchildren arrive, the extended family becomes either stronger or more frayed. Personalities can clash. Expectations can diverge widely. Geographical and financial differences become more of a factor. If you live close by and provide childcare, will you resent the "swoop in" Glamma who comes loaded with expensive gifts you couldn't afford? Age and health are two other huge factors. If the doctor tells you not to carry heavy loads, let's hope Fitness Nana doesn't flaunt her bulging biceps and six-pack abs.

No two sets of grandparents will relate in exactly the same way to either their own child or their child's child. And grandparents who are sensitive to the needs, interests, and values of the other people who claim the same child will strengthen the ties that bind you to each other.

Grandchildren create a new "third thing," with the potential to bond all members of the extended family together. With everyone loving the new little ones, the time is right for keen observation, noting the other grandparents' strengths and preferred styles of interacting. For example, Owen and Julia have benefited so much from Granddad Clayton's gift for storytelling and his anchorman's deep voice. Grandma Nancy's sharp legal mind helps her ask the children good questions, and her gift for gift-giving shows up in Christmas photos with the whole family decked out in long winter caps like Saint Nick's. Similarly, Lydia has listened attentively as her Grammie sits at her grand piano and plays *Moonlight Sonata* or the soundtrack from her favorite movie. When Pops uses a new puzzle as the opportunity to teach Lydia about shapes and numbers, you can feel his lifelong devotion to mathematics showing through. Lydia feels it too.

At the end of his long autobiographical poem, William Wordsworth declares to his fellow poet Coleridge, "What we have loved, others will love, and we will teach them how." How fortunate young children are if they are surrounded by a whole team of people who share different loves with them. Each of us can help build the team simply by being mindful—searching for the gifts and delights of the others and freely expressing our own.

As you observe the interactions of the "other" grandparents in your family, you will likely respond more naturally to some than to others. If you have a basic agreement on spiritual and political values, you will sense it early. Enjoy the harmony and work together to pass along those values to the next generation. If you disagree sharply, you have all the more reason to search for common ground while still remaining true to your own beliefs. You might build trust and tolerance for differences by focusing on a safer kind of conflict—what kind of athletic team, or genre of music, or barbecue sauce do you like best? And why?

None of us has an advanced degree in grandparenting. What we know we have learned from the wisest of our own elders and from the sources of wisdom we trust in all things: our sacred texts, learned teachers, and intimate friends. We can add our grandchildren's other grandparents to that list. They bring strengths and gifts and traditions that will form these little ones' lives. Loving the same children, we are on the same team. Caring for our shared grandchildren, we are bound together.

Suggestions for Grandparents

1. Invite your grandchildren's other grandparents to a conversation, either in writing or by phone. Here are some questions you might choose to ask:
   - What memories do you have of your own grandparents? Are they helpful role models? Mixed? Nonexistent?

- How did your own parents interact with your children? Did their degree of involvement change over time?
- What have you learned from our shared grandchild or grandchildren?
- What gifts or values do you hope to give to them?
- What concerns do you have that you feel open to sharing?
- How can we work together?

2. We might all benefit from the practices of good fundraising. Take notes! Today we can do that with the Notes app on a smartphone. Just put in the name of a person you want to relate to (the other grandparents, in this case) and jot down the names of pets, hobbies, and a myriad of other preferences. When you can ask about Two Speed or Allegra by name instead of "How's your cat?" you show that you've been paying attention. In the end, we all hope someone has noticed our unique way of being in the world. And noticing is a great gift to give our grandchildren.

10

HEIRLOOM EGGS

Shirley

You don't ever let go of the thread.
—William Stafford, "The Way It Is"

I stood at the doorway to Grandma's kitchen, holding my blanket. I was a three-year-old staying with grandparents to keep my measles germs away from my baby brother at home. Yellow light filled the room, making Grandma's kind face even warmer.

Why do I remember this morning so long ago? Was it because Grandma and I were alone? Perhaps. Usually, the kitchen I visited was full of uncles and aunts and cousins. Was it because of the words spoken? No, because I have to reconstruct the words in my imagination. But the energy of love and the quality of attention that day penetrated deeply into memory.

"Would you like breakfast?" Grandma asked. I nodded. Ordinarily, she would have made fried eggs and toast or just poured a bowl of cornflakes. This morning, however, she scooped a single egg into a pan of water. While waiting for it to boil, she pulled a piece of bread out of a bag and placed it in the toaster. Then she went to the cupboard, searching for just the right cup.

She found a large white mug and placed it next to the stove. Using a slotted spoon, she pulled the egg out of the water. She let it sit on top of the spoon, cooling, for a minute or so. Then she held the egg between her thumb and index finger and, with her other hand, hit it sharply with a knife, using a plate to catch the two halves. She exhaled, slightly smiling, when she saw the egg inside. It would slide easily into the cup.

"It's not runny. It's not hard. It's just right," she said quietly. She looked at me as though to say, *You will do this too someday*.

"Now take this toast and tear off little snipples as though you were cutting with scissors. Put them in this cup."

I complied, eager to be part of such a precise and important project. While I tore the toast, Grandma dug the egg out of the split shell with a spoon. She took a fork and pressed toast and egg together until all the pieces became part of each other, moist and warm. Brown crumbs rimmed the cup and spilled over onto the oilcloth-covered table. Specks of yellow yolk, like solid sunshine, filled the dappled cup to the top. She pushed the masterpiece in front of me.

I don't think we paused to say grace, but grace is exactly what I felt. That soft-boiled egg still ranks among my all-time favorite meals.

Looking back, I see that day as an emblem of the way my two very different Hershey grandparents loved me and how the women of my family turned love from a feeling into a fact. Though we lived only seven miles apart, I mostly saw Grandma and Grandpa at church. They were there every week. Grandpa sat on the left side facing the pulpit. Grandma sat across the aisle with the other women. Both of them wore the plain garb of the Mennonite church. His dark coat jacket was buttoned all the way up, covering his white shirt and tiny black bow tie. When he entered his pew, he kissed the man beside him with the "holy kiss" or "kiss of peace."

Grandma's dress was long and included an extra layer, called a cape, which concealed her commodious bosom. She sat with women her age near the front. She also gave the holy kiss to her neighbor.

My grandfather was known as the candy man. After the service, I proudly skipped to Grandpa's spot at the back of the church, usually with four or five other kids trailing behind me, all of us hoping he would fish something wonderful—like cellophane-wrapped butterscotch drops, peppermint lozenges, or sticks of gum—out of his pocket. Grandpa pretended not to have anything, then reached deeper, watching us catch our collective breath when we saw peppermint gum. He enjoyed his popularity.

Grandma did not dote on her grandchildren, partly because she had eighteen of them! I don't remember her cuddling me or reading stories or coming to my school activities. Here's what I do remember about Grandma. She loved her family with her hands rather than her words. She was always making something—canning, baking, sewing, knitting, crocheting, gardening—or cleaning so that she could start one of these projects all over again. She made an afghan for every grandchild. As a member of the sewing circle at church, she knitted comforters and stitched quilts for refugees and homeless people.

Grandma Hershey took her turn hosting her widowed mother, my great-grandma Snyder, in her home, returning the love she had been given as a child and honoring the one who taught her that hands were sacred instruments of grace. The brown-spotted hands of both Grandma and Great-Grandma bore marks of heavy labor in gardens and fields. They also formed a matriarchal lineage: they were the queen mother and the queen of the home place, the farm that had sustained many generations.

Great-Grandma Snyder's special talent was making braided rugs. Often when staying with Grandma Hershey, she would take up the table in the dining room with a large wool floor rug partially finished and invite children to watch as she wound three strands of wool into tight and strong cords, ready to be stitched into an oval or circle.

My favorite heirloom from her is a much smaller mat. It sits under the hurricane lamp in our guest bedroom. Oval in shape, the slim mat serves the function of a doily. Its green, gold, tan, and brown colors have faded with exposure to sunlight over the years, weathering them like the layers of rock exposed on a mountain. Bending closer, I can see the handiwork of an artist. Each little braid is tightly pressed against the next. There are no signs of endings or beginnings and no bulges, just a continuous stream of three strands of nylon—recycled women's hosiery!—tightly woven together, not easily broken.

Someday, far into the future, a little child may show up at my adult grandchild's kitchen door, ready to be shown a new gift. My work now is to remember stories worth sharing, make new ones, and pass along a few well-chosen heirlooms.

I'll be visiting granddaughter Lydia soon. I plan to ask her if she wants to make snipples of toast and see me turn one egg into two. As we make our own soft-boiled egg, I will tell her about my Grandma Hershey. I'm pretty sure yellow light will stream through the window.

Suggestions for Grandparents

1. Take time in silence to reflect on particular memories from long ago. Reach for the earliest ones you can remember. Pull on the thread of an early impression to see what surfaces. Keep a journal close by and jot down anything that comes up in your mind. A color? A smell? A feeling? Almost any thread can lead you back in time. Write what you remember. Shape it into a story.

2. Test your story with a grandchild. Try to find a good opening that arouses curiosity. ("What is your favorite meal?" "Did you ever eat anything that made your stomach feel better after you were sick?") Then follow the questions they ask. You might even remember more because a child's focus takes you out of the fog that develops over time.

3. Do you have physical heirlooms from your own grandparents or great-grandparents? These can be carefully handled with grandchildren and will almost inevitably lead to a story. The tactile and other sensory experiences of the past will make a lasting impression.

11

FRUITS AND NUTS
AND ALL THINGS FRESH

Marilyn

Eat real food.
Not too much.
Mostly vegetables.

—Michael Pollan

My daughter and I have laughed more than a few times over
a story from her babysitting days. She frequently cared for a
child whose mother gave particularly rigorous attention to
her daughter's diet: no sugar, no processed foods, no preservatives, nothing in packages or out of gumball machines.

When the child's fifth birthday approached, her mother planned her first birthday party with friends, knowing there had to come a time for the long-postponed introduction to birthday cake. When she asked the little girl what food she would like to serve to her friends, she replied, "Do you think we could have spinach treats?"

I never heard how that party came off. Either the unsuspecting friends had their first spinach treats, or the little girl had her first cake. (I leave you to consider which is more likely.) But I have watched our kids navigate a world of food choices for themselves and their children in which processed and colorfully packaged foods, many saturated with high-fructose corn syrup and artificial flavorings, have lined grocery shelves at child's eye level. When little boys gather to play T-ball at the park, the "snack shack" is open at the edge of the field, selling chips and soda and candy. Their holidays are interspersed with numerous birthday parties—parties at which, I'm guessing, spinach treats are not being served.

For a variety of reasons, most having to do with food industry lobbies, average per-capita sugar consumption in the United States has gone up from 2 pounds a year two hundred years ago to about 152 pounds a year. Obesity and diabetes are now being described as public-health crises. It's hard not to think about these facts when it's time for "treats."

It's not primarily up to me, of course, to control my grandchildren's daily diets. But I can, and do, broach the subject with their parents on occasion. We all inhabit the same food system, where the words *Healthy Choice* can be found on packages of what Michael Pollan called "food-like substances." Pollan's three rules for healthy eating have been a helpful point of reference in those conversations: "Eat real food. Not too much. Mostly vegetables." Real food, by his definition, generally comes unpackaged and can be found in the produce section or at the local farmer's market. But according to recent statistics, about 23.5 million Americans live in "food deserts"—areas where access to fresh, healthy fruits and vegetables is very limited. And even for those who do have that access, the convenience of packaged and processed foods is often compelling when both parents are working full-time, as many are.

This is where grandparents often come into the picture. I don't take care of my grandchildren daily, as many grandparents do. But I do live close enough to them that, once a week, I pick them up from school and give them snacks, lunch on "early release" days, and sometimes dinner, if we're lucky enough to have them for the evening. So we have the inevitable conversation about snacks and treats and what's "healthy."

It's a conversation to have with care. I don't want to undermine their parents' efforts to feed them properly, though, in some instances, my choices would be different. But I can talk about why we don't keep candy around, or why we don't buy soda or keep ice cream in the freezer. Having that conversation with a four-year-old can go something like this:

"Grandma, I'm hungry. Could I have a cookie?"

"I don't have any cookies. But I can make apple slices with cinnamon."

"Do you have any candy?"

"Nope. But we can make a plate of pineapple slices and blueberries on toothpicks and have it out on the patio."

For the sake of full disclosure, I should say we do have hot chocolate (made from unsweetened cocoa powder so I can control the amount of sugar included) and occasional home-made cookies. (I've found that reducing the sugar in a cookie recipe is almost never noticeable enough to excite comment.) But my main point here is that even small children can be engaged in conversation about what happens to food in your body, where it comes from, and the most fun and colorful ways to prepare fruits and vegetables. I'd like to help equip them to make healthy and responsible choices as they grow to make more of their own choices about how to eat. I'd like to help them begin, even while they're small, to recognize how the earth provides what we need, how many people are involved in bringing food to our table, and what "enough" feels like. I'd like to model for them that food is worth talking about as we choose and prepare it; such conversations could make a big difference in habit formation.

I haven't offered them spinach treats on their birthdays—yet. But they like small squares of spinach quiche, and they don't seem to mind a mix of spinach and berries in their smoothies. The ones old enough to stand on a kitchen stool have their own aprons, and we cook together. They love measuring cups and long wooden spoons. They get to stir and pour and sprinkle spices. Grandma's house may not be a sugar source, but most days, we manage to offer satisfying alternatives.

Suggestions for Grandparents

1. The food conversation is an important one to have. Some sources I've found helpful are Michael Pollan's several

books about food, the many TED Talks about food that can be found on YouTube, and documentaries like *Forks over Knives* (2011), *Fed Up* (2014), and *The Biggest Little Farm* (2019). Good books about nutrition written for children include *Good Enough to Eat* by Lizzy Rockwell and a cookbook for kids, *Eat Your Greens, Reds, Yellows, and Purples* by DK.

2. Cooking and baking, even with small children, can be a ritual everyone looks forward to. Making bread with small kids isn't hard if ingredients are prepared ahead of time—and the kneading is the best part! It's worth investing in several small loaf pans for this purpose.

3. "Field trips" to a local farmer's market can be organized as scavenger hunts and followed by a festive lunch prepared together. Tearing lettuce, mashing avocados, and washing carrots are all tasks in which very small children can take remarkable pleasure.

12

MICKEY MOUSE PANCAKES

Shirley

Four and twenty blackbirds
Baked in a pie. . . .
Along came a blackbird
And snipped off her nose.

—Mother Goose

As any nursery rhyme or parenting magazine can tell you, the kitchen is a dangerous place. It's also a great learning laboratory. So when we head to the kitchen with our grandchildren, the goal is to keep their noses, hands, and toes intact while chopping, scraping, mixing, and stirring.

Grammie and Pops, three-year-old Lydia's other grandparents, gave her a handmade gift that feeds her curiosity and her vision of life as a sous-chef. It's a simple wooden tower that raises her about two feet. It also provides a waist-high cage that gives her a little stability when she wants to be part of the action. Usually, it sits beside the fridge, but when there is a project, Lydia drags it to the island and climbs inside.

During one recent visit, we used the tower for multiple projects.

SATURDAY MORNING PANCAKES

"Good morning, Lydia. I think Mommy and Daddy are still sleeping. Would you like to come down to the kitchen with me to make pancakes?"

"Yes!"

This was a win already because usually, when I try to get her out of bed and take her to the potty, she says, "Go away, Grandma. I want Mommy." Nothing like a three-year-old to teach you your place! This time, however, the idea of making pancakes overrode her personal preference. Novelty is her thing right now. Daily rituals are not.

After we turned the corner on the wooden landing to the kitchen, Lydia headed straight for her tower. I picked up a stainless-steel bowl, a milk carton, the flour canister, an egg, and a box of baking powder.

"Do you know what these things are?"

"Ingredients!" she sang out. She clearly knows the drill. I placed the measuring spoons in front of her.

"Do you want to help me measure a teaspoon of baking powder?" Her hands were over mine immediately.

"Watch this!" I guided her to scrape off the mound on the teaspoon along the edge of the box to make it firm and smooth. Her eyes widened as she dumped the exact amount into the bowl. She sprinkled in the flour, poured the milk, and made the first tentative crack in each egg.

When the batter was finished, Lydia was content to have me guide her in pouring a big circle into the middle of the hot iron skillet and then immediately adding two small circles for the "ears."

"See the bubbles? They tell us Mickey is ready to flip over!" Together we lifted our masterpiece without tearing it, while Lydia kept her distance from the hot skillet.

I'm not sure who was prouder of our lovely light-brown pancake, Lydia or me. Both of us were full of what Lydia likes to call "energies."

PLAY-DOH

A few days later, Lydia was back in the kitchen tower for another project. This time we were making our own Play-Doh in Lydia's favorite color, purple. And my daughter Kate was helping.

The simple ingredients were no harder to combine than the pancakes, and they yielded a lovely warm mound of dough ready for food coloring. We started with purple, the favorite, but then blue looked pretty good too. And how could we leave out pink?

Watching Lydia and her mom stirring the color into the dough, so close to each other in a kitchen full of knives, flames, and heavy pots, I was grateful once again for the imagination of the person who made a tower to help keep a child safe and equalize her position in the kitchen and for

Grammie and Pops, her other grandparents, who thought to give this towering gift.

Suggestions for Grandparents

1. Are you handy with a hammer, nails, and a paintbrush? The kitchen tower would be an excellent project for a grandparent who likes to make gifts rather than buy them. If you live close by, your grandchild might even want to "help" you paint or glue or hammer.

2. Mickey Mouse pancakes can be as simple as pouring three circles of batter onto a hot skillet as described earlier. Lydia was delighted with these, and we kept the sugar level low. Of course, you can make a Mickey or Minnie face with chocolate chips or raisins too. Just plain pancakes with cut-up strawberries or blueberries are also special treats.

3. Play-Doh recipes abound on the internet. Here is the one we used, which is posted on the website of the Pittsburgh Toy Lending Library. We made a half batch, which is still a generous amount.

Play-Doh Recipe

Ingredients
- 5 cups water
- ½ cup vegetable or canola oil
- 4 cups flour
- 1 cup salt
- 2 tablespoons cream of tartar
- food coloring (optional)

Directions

1. Combine ingredients in a large pot. Mix well.
2. Warm up mixture on stove over medium to medium-high heat, stirring frequently.
3. When mixture reaches a thick, doughy consistency, remove from heat.
4. Let dough cool. Knead by hand or mix with a stand mixer. Add food coloring as desired.

13

THE GRANDMA THEY'LL NEVER KNOW

Marilyn

We all carry, inside us, people who came before us.
—Liam Callanan, *The Cloud Atlas*

I have been quite moved at several weddings in which the ceremony included acknowledging, by name, family members and close friends who had died before they could participate in the joy of the occasion. After each name was read, a designated person responded, "*Presente,*" in Spanish, as the custom comes from Latin American movements for justice. They are among us, we are reminded—here in spirit, here in the legacy of their love, here in the stories we tell about them and on their behalf.

I think of that lovely custom often as I watch our two youngest grandchildren. Their fathers are my beloved step-sons, whose mother died when they were eleven and sixteen. Her dearest wish was to see her children into adulthood. She would have loved to see her children's children into the world. Sometimes as I watch Soren, looking so much like his dad, dancing with delight in the sand, or watch Ella, curled comfortably near the big dogs who think they're her guard-ians, I think of their grandmother and murmur, "*Presente*."

Her picture hangs in a family gallery. She will always be, for them, young and beautiful and mythic. She will be a sto-ried presence. As they grow older, they will come to recog-nize the ache their fathers feel from time to time because they can't know her.

Ella's other grandmother died shortly before she was born. There are two photos in the hallway outside of her bed-room of two women—Susie and Diane—whose stories and images and DNA will be hers. I'm the one who gets to be her "Grandma Mac," but I'm aware that I can't "replace" them—nothing will. I'm aware that I can't even "represent" them, in the sense that their parents and grandfathers are the ones whose memories will be richest and most immediate. I'm aware, sometimes, of flashes of jealousy of the young, lively, beautiful images of the absent grandmothers on the wall as I make my own very human mistakes. I'm aware, too, of the honor it is to be so fully authorized by our sons and their wives to be the grandma I am. I'm what they've got.

Life shuffles the deck, and time and loss reconstitute the family circles. Other friends and neighbors step into grandparenting roles for both Soren and Ella, and I see how blessed they are with a circle of elders because their parents seek and value that for them. Much has been written about the language we bring to recombinant family groups and reassigned familial roles. Most of us are aware of how unhelpful it is to distinguish between stepparents and "real" parents, for instance. "Biological" mother or grandmother seems too clinical. I like the term *birth mother*, both in describing my relationship to my own daughters, who have a stepmother, and in describing my stepsons' mother, who will always hold that place of honor. Sometimes simply "your other grandma" may be an adequate and simple way to acknowledge that there is more to the finely woven web of relationship we're held in than meets the eye.

For there are always others. I wish my children could have had time to know my grandmother. I wish I had known the one who died before she met me. It's good to find moments to tell the stories that link these little ones to the grandmothers they'll never know in this life. It's also good simply to remember them quietly, whispering as we watch their children's children jumping in autumn leaves, "¡*Presente!*"

Suggestions for Grandparents

1. As children grow, it's helpful to consider which stories in the repertoire are yours to tell. If you happen to have known those who have died, how does your point of view add complexity and texture to those stories? There is a difference between loving commemoration and enshrinement. It's good to model memory and commemoration

for them and also to avoid sentimentality or sanitizing. In what ways can you give permission to laugh and wonder, leaving the unknown unknown? It's good, too, to learn to be comfortably silent as others tell stories that aren't yours to tell. This can be its own spiritual discipline.

2. One of several lovely books for children about remembering the dead is Pat Mora's *Remembering Day* (also available in a Spanish edition, *El día de los muertos*). Anniversaries like birthdays or death days can be observed simply by reading a story or lighting a candle, letting it remain lit in a safe place as a shining presence throughout the day.

PART II
THE WORLD
AROUND THEM

It is the responsibility of every adult . . . to make sure that children hear what we have learned from the lessons of life and to hear over and over that we love them and that they are not alone.

—Marian Wright Edelman, *The Measure of Our Success: A Letter to My Children and Yours*

14

THE GIFT OF PLAY

Shirley

Reide, reide, geili
Alle Schtunn en Meili;
Geht's iwwer der Schtumbe,
Fallt's Bobbli nunner.

Ride, ride, little horse
Every hour a little mile;
When it goes over the stump,
The baby falls down!
  —"Reide, Reide, Geili," old Pennsylvania Dutch song

Where did your ancestors come from? No matter your
answer, you can be sure that those cultures had lullabies and

lap bounces. With a little research, you might be able to find one your grandbabies will love.

My ancestors all came to America from Switzerland and Germany in the eighteenth century. They brought with them a few traditions that have persisted even over ten generations: foods such as pork and sauerkraut, a few untranslatable expressions like *Schtrublich* (wild, ungovernable hair) and *Schusslich* (restless, sloppy behavior), and a song to sing to a baby (see epigraph to this chapter).

The song contains elements similar to the well-known English lullaby: "Rock-a-bye Baby in the treetop, / when the wind blows the cradle will rock. / When the bough breaks, the cradle will fall, / and down will come cradle, baby, and all." Both songs end with the baby falling, which seems a strange and frightening thing for both parents and children to sing about! The baby falling seems to be a universal theme in many cultures. There are Spanish, Haitian, and even ancient Babylonian examples.

Why would songs like these continue when everything else—technology, child-rearing advice, language, religion— changes? Here are some of my hunches.

First, the song names our deepest fear when new life has entered a family. The baby, so tiny, so vulnerable, might "fall down." Comfort from this fear comes from the little horse or the cradle, which cannot prevent the fall but nevertheless represents a kind of shelter. The baby can remount the little horse or be placed back into the cradle. The song is always sung more than once, underscoring the ultimate safety of the baby. Fear is there, but so is love and comfort. The baby—and the caregiver too—are learning resilience. Having named the worst that can happen, they offer arms of embrace and a song.

Beyond the reverse psychology, however, are two more elemental drives: sleep and play. They can best be understood when we notice the role of motion in singing.

In the case of "Rock-a-bye Baby," the motion is rocking, often in a rocking chair, and the goal is not play but relaxation. Even while singing about the bough breaking, the singer continues gentle rocking. The voice is soft. In the past, the person singing was usually a mother or grandmother, though a song in a father or grandfather's deeper voice is its own particular and irreplaceable gift.

In the case of "Reide, Reide, Geili" however, the motion starts with bouncing the baby on both knees while holding the baby's hands, as though the knees are horses. The goal is fun. The baby giggles then squeals with frightful delight when the knees part and the baby drops in the last verse. If the baby or toddler can speak, one of the first words is usually "Again!" Baby climbs up on the little horse and off they go, only to tumble and recover, tumble and recover.

The song works for any adult, but in the case of my family, it was the choice of the fathers and grandfathers. The men were patriarchs, sure that their authority to command and discipline came directly from God. But when there was a baby in the house—which was often—they softened. Often siblings, cousins, aunts, and uncles were present, too, to watch the fathers and the grandfathers remember how to play. We played with them, loving the laughter and joy that was too often missing in ordinary time.

I can still see my grandfather, a patriarch to his own children but more like a patron to his grandchildren, gleefully bouncing my brother and cousins. My father didn't copy my grandfather in everything, but he, too, sang the song to me and my siblings. By the time my own children came along, Stuart and I could both remember the words "Reide, reide, Geili." And the tune. And the fall through the knees. We couldn't recall the rest of the words, but with the help of the internet, we have now recovered the whole song in the original dialect in time to sing them to Lydia.

Peter Gray, a Boston College professor who has studied the evolutionary impact of play and laments its decline (TEDx talk, "The Decline of Play"), says, "Play is God's gift." He also believes that the current educational system in America could benefit from much more free play. Before him, Maria Montessori built an entire curriculum around the centrality of play. "Children become like the things they love," she said, always thinking about how children could teach themselves in the presence of water tables and blocks and other elements they can construct and manipulate. In choosing what to love, they find peace.

Grandparents have important roles in this mixture of old and new wisdom about play. What can grandparents do? They can remember and tell stories.

After the babies are too big to be dandled on the knees, they will enjoy stories about how you played when you were a child. Do any of these words evoke any memories? Mud pies, tea parties, water, measuring cups, pots and pans, minnows, tadpoles, lightning bugs, Ball Dome jars, dandelions, barefoot, seashells, climbing trees, garden, hay bales, puppies, kittens, baby mice, forts and tunnels, the corner store, Lincoln Logs, Tinkertoys, an open fire hydrant. If not, what do you remember about play? The best memories connect us across generations to the natural world and to imagination.

Sometimes old-fashioned toys can also evoke memories of play: chalk for hopscotch, a rope for jumping and jump-rope rhymes, jacks, pick-up sticks, and roller skates. Anything you loved yourself and want to teach your grandchild will become a treasured memory with an increased chance of transfer to more generations in the future. We were able to purchase a marble roller like the one I remember in my grandparents' house. Fashioned by a local artisan from four different types of wood, the roller attracts children of all ages. As soon as they hear the roar of marbles going around the bend, speeding into the little cup, they begin to design new games of competition, cooperation, and chance.

As soon as you know you will be a grandparent, you can begin with your dreamy recollections of play. You can reclaim, through memory, your own play spaces, play skills, and body memories of play. Then life itself will take you on a path to play with your grandchild. You can also take your current hobbies and find ways to introduce grandchildren to them. Recently I talked with a teenage boy wearing a camera around his neck. I asked if he had any teachers or mentors. "My grandfather," he said with the kind of quiet joy that indicated respect and devotion.

A few years ago, I was walking in a park next to my pre-school granddaughter Julia. "Look," I said. "Grass clippings!" She looked up at me, quizzically.

"Watch," I said as I knelt down in the recently mowed grass. Scooping up the clippings into piles, I arranged them into squares.

"What do you think I am making?" I asked.

"A house!" she said triumphantly, kneeling down without an invitation and scooping more clippings into piles and rectangles. Soon I was telling her a story of our long recesses at Fairland Elementary School in the 1950s and about the many hours of fun we had making grass houses on the playground. As I reached back in time, I could hear the wooden softball bats cracking, the rusty chains of the swings creaking, and the seesaw thudding after the riders jumped off. So much playing. Over on the other side of the playground, girls in skirts with starched petticoats were singing, "Down in the meadow."

Next time Julia comes to visit, we'll go outside to make fairy houses, a modern version of the grass houses of the playground. At the edge of the yard, a huge meadow stretches out over the hillside. Maybe we'll sing an old song with our own words: "Down in the meadow where the green grass grows, / There sat Julia as sweet as a rose, / She sang. She sang. She sang so sweet. / Along came Grandma and swept her off her feet. / How many kisses did she get? / One / Two / Three . . ."

Julia is likely at this point to blurt out, "A million!" And I am likely to catch her as she runs away: kissing her, tossing her, and—almost—letting her fall.

Suggestions for Grandparents

1. "A Smooth Road" is a lap-bounce song in English that recollects most of the elements of "Reide, Reide, Geili" and adds a few more. It progresses from "smooth" swaying on the knee to "rough" bouncing to the inevitable "fall" through a hole. You can find examples on YouTube.
2. To explore the role of lullabies in all cultures, the internet is again your friend. You can find a World Lullabies channel

on YouTube and many fascinating articles documenting the powerful impact on babies regardless of the language.

3. Social scientists Peter Gray and Stuart Brown have written books, established websites, and given TED Talks that interpret important research in the field of play. Also see *Free Play: The Power of Improvisation in Life and Art* by Stephen Nachmanovitch—a book to read for our own, as well as our grandchildren's, sake.

4. Biographies of Maria Montessori and her own published works are inspiring examples of how a philosophy of learning based on play arose. Montessori.org online brings you up-to-date on the most recent applications of Montessori's curriculum.

15

STUFF BETTER THAN TOYS?

Shirley

Stuff to Save and Recycle in New Ways

- Cardboard boxes: big ones from appliances, or other sizes stashed in the garage or basement
- Oatmeal containers
- Cardboard tubes: toilet paper, paper towel, and gift wrap
- Paint, glue, glitter, tape, scissors, markers
- Clean glass jars with lids
- Clean takeout containers
- Construction paper and scrap paper

- Little scraps of wrapping paper, tissue paper, and gift bags
- Sheets of stickers and labels mailed to you from non-profit groups
- Fabric scraps

Stuff That Can Be Turned into Forts, Tunnels, and Drum Sets

- Blankets and sheets
- Chairs, sofas, and tables
- Cushions and pillows
- Pots, pans, and wooden spoons
- Sieves, sifters, and a rolling pin

Stuff You May Have Forgotten You Had

- Costume jewelry you never wear
- Little bags and nice boxes that held fine jewelry
- Buttons and pins you picked up from travels or from awards or gifts
- Little bottles of shampoo and body lotion from hotels

Stuff in the Back of Your Closet

- Gowns and scarves
- Ties and cuff links
- Silver or gold sandals
- Beach bags full of beach towels
- Boots

Stuff on Your Desk

- Old cards without envelopes and envelopes without cards
- Paper clips and bookmarks
- Pens, pencils, and tablets
- Photos
- Rulers and measuring tape

Stuff for Gardening

- Seeds
- Bulbs
- Work gloves
- Any tool made of plastic or wood

Stuff Your Own Children Loved That You Saved

- Tea sets, Legos, blocks, balls, and games
- Paper dolls
- Books
- Record albums and cassette tapes

Stuff in Your Junk Drawer

- Rubber bands
- Pens, pencils, and sticky notes
- Paper clips
- Magnets

Suggestions for Grandparents

1. Having grandchildren helps you look at your house in a new way. A quick internet search can give you additional ideas for what to do with common household items—for example, how to make a ball out of rubber bands. This is an easy and fun activity to do with children when they visit, or you could do it while watching a movie and then send them the ball.

2. If you do not live close enough to have your grandchildren in your home often, you can create care packages for them made up of a mixture of new toys and treats and "found objects" from your house. You could send these packages on holidays like Valentine's Day or Arbor Day.

3. Consider sending a package for the sheer joy of giving them a surprise. You could include instructions for other things they can do on their end: a scavenger hunt, picture to draw, book to make, letter to write, cookies to bake (along with a recipe).

4. You can help grandchildren look at their apartment or house in a new way too. You can create a survey form for them:

   - How many windows does your home have?
   - How many doors?
   - How many trees are within twenty yards of your house?
   - How many chairs?
   - How many weeds can you pull out of the garden or flower bed?
   - Where is your house or apartment number located?
   - How many house plants?

16

A KING, A PRINCE, AND A PILE OF PILLOWS

Marilyn

King True lived on a mountain
That no one else could climb
Except his brother, good Prince Brave
Who came from time to time.

Each of my daughters has parenting habits that make me smile—they're so characteristic of who they are. One is a natural organizer; her spreadsheets and shopping lists serve her well on her way from holding down a demanding job to evenings of holding her babies. One settles her little people in her art space with age-appropriate materials while she paints, convinced that if you can hold an implement, you can be a maker. One lets a lot of the outdoors inside—sticks and twigs, small stone collections, and even an occasional bug in a matchbox. She is also easygoing about the uses of furniture: what's a sofa for if not to be a fort or a castle?

On one visit, I was stopped at the door of our daughter's family room by a pronouncement delivered by a small boy on a large pile of sofa cushions and pillows: "I am King True." He brandished what I took to be a sword, though it might have been a scepter. Then he gestured at the bemused little brother who sat in a saggy diaper at the foot of the mountain: "And this is Prince Brave."

"Is that your mountain?" I inquired.

"Yes!" he declared, indicating with a sweeping gesture that his territory actually included the entire family room and possibly the kitchen.

"Does Prince Brave live there too?" I asked, still in the doorway, waiting for an invitation to enter if I was friend, not foe.

He looked at me as though he found it hard to believe I'd asked such a silly question. "Prince Brave is my brother!" he replied. Duh. Of course he lived there.

Finding a seat at the edge of their property, I chatted with the queen mother, who was calmly making mac and cheese and laughing. She seemed quite unperturbed by the number of household items that had been pressed into service, including cushions from nearby chairs, table runners, books (for steps), supplies from the food cupboard, and even one sturdy end table on its side. King True had a trove: he and Prince Brave were well supplied.

I admire my daughter's easy acceptance of the fact that children will climb, soil, spill, and otherwise diminish the half-life of household items one might ideally want to keep clean and in good repair. She and her husband aren't so affluent as to take the purchase of a new sofa lightly. Still, it seems perfectly clear to her that children need generous access to things that allow imaginative play. If that means the furniture is a bit worn, or that stain remover has to be kept as handy as the salt, it's well worth the cost. It's what furniture is for—and sheets and bowls and (as long as it's not a weapon) the rolling pin.

This particular daughter loves theater. She especially values the training she received in improv classes, in which the first rule was to "say yes" to whatever happens on stage and see what may develop. She has brought that theory home. Wherever she can, she says yes. Yes, you may use that. You may climb on it. You may jump into it. You may pull it from the cupboard. You may take it apart and we'll put it back together when you're done. She has boundaries, and the boys know what they are, but there's generous play space inside those boundaries.

I remembered, watching King True and Prince Brave, my own fantasy play as a child. Our parents weren't desperately poor, but they lived, as so many do, paycheck to paycheck. So my mother, though imaginative and cheerful, was careful. A child of the Depression, she was attentive to the costs involved in maintaining or, when absolutely necessary, replacing household items. Her permission, I'm sure, came after a quick reckoning: How much would it cost to replace the sheets if we tore them? What kinds of breakage could

be included in the budget? We weren't destructive or careless kids, but things happen.

When our grandchildren come to our place, I find my
thoughts moving between my mother and daughter as I try
to find the right balance point for our household rules: which
chairs are OK to climb on, what needs to be moved out of
reach, how much access to give to cupboards, what they may
freely explore and when they have to ask. Our house isn't as
babyproofed as their own homes, though we've made efforts.
I'm becoming used to the quick inspection before they come,
quietly putting away the more fragile pieces or the ones that
are harder to clean, and I've foraged in more than a few
thrift stores for objects they can put to their own surprising
purposes.

What I have learned again, partly from my own children,
is that if you have members of a royal family in your house,
they will very likely need a mountain, possibly a fortress
or a cave or a corral for dragons, and lookout towers that look
a lot like tall chairs and tents and walking sticks and a few
musical instruments—pots and wooden spoons will do. It's
good to have those around.

Suggestions for Grandparents

1. If possible, have a cupboard or trunk in your house that
   visiting grandkids know is theirs. It can be stashed with
   supplies they're familiar with, and it's also a good place to
   plant a surprise now and then.
2. Modeling imaginative play by speculating with grandchildren about possible uses of a sieve or a whisk or an

oatmeal carton or even a lampshade—here's where I'd recommend a spare from the thrift store—is not only fun for them; it's good for us too. Such play helps us get out of our own groove and scrutinize our ordinary objects in new terms, considering their excellent possibilities.

17

EVERY CHILD IS AN ARTIST

Shirley

Every child is an artist until he's told he's not an artist.
—John Lennon, interview in *Time* magazine, 1969

I'm looking at a drawing in my journal created by two-year-old Lydia. Now that we are no longer living in the same place, I can study the drawing and remember the experience of watching her, a child artist, at work.

First, she smiled and looked up at me, pen in hand, journal in her lap. She is only allowed to use a pen when she has adult supervision, so just holding this writing instrument was a triumph of two-year-old will.

She carefully made a big circle. Inside it, she drew two smaller circles.

"Eyes," she said.

Then another circle below, presumably the nose. No mouth.

"Grandma," she said as she executed one last flourish, wavy lines around the whole body and a set of squiggly arms and legs underneath. I rather liked her result. I looked a bit like a diva.

She didn't just use her hand and fingers to draw; she moved her whole body with every stroke. Her delight and fearlessness fueled her full-body engagement.

Watching her, I remembered seeing an internet quote purported to be from Picasso: "It took me four years to learn how to paint like Rafael, but a lifetime to learn how to paint like a child." It made intuitive sense.

A few months earlier, when all three grandchildren were together, they took turns doing digital painting on my iPad. All of them love to draw. Watching them, I remembered getting lost in drawing when I was a child.

Julia, age seven, has made art a passion and yet handles it so lightly. She fills books with drawings and stickers, using them in ways only she could think of. She can fill up a page with animals as fast as she tosses "stuffies" into her closet. Executing her brush strokes with both confidence and curiosity, she dashes off one painting and starts another immediately. She never pauses to admire her work, nor does she scratch her head and wonder what to paint next. She just goes for it! Somehow I think Picasso would approve.

Owen, almost nine, has entered a new phase of artistic exploration. His personality is calm. He likes precision. I gave him an old camera a few years ago, and he has started taking pictures. Somehow he discovered digital filters and now turns our everyday lives into paintings.

Owen snapped a photo of Julia and me looking at the iPad together. He transformed the Costa Rican fish and the Russian doll in the background using a black-and-white filter. When he draws freestyle these days, Owen likes to stop action and add detail. He also has to fight for his turn at the iPad.

My grandchildren have reignited my own artistic yearnings. By paying close attention to children and their work, I am getting closer to the time when I return to making art.

When I try, however, I hesitate. What should I draw? What brush stroke should I use? Do those colors go together? I've lived in my head a long time, and I have focused on language rather than image. But maybe there's hope. Maybe someday we will all paint together.

Hey, if Picasso needed a lifetime to learn how to draw like a child, I had better get started!

Suggestions for Grandparents

1. Art supplies are inducements to creativity, and the smells of newly sharpened pencils and a recently opened box of crayons can transport adults and children alike to new places in their imaginations. When you create a space for art in your home or take presents to children, you can't go wrong with art supplies. Your grandchild will take in the sensory delights of color, smell, and closeness to you and will always remember them. You, in turn, might remember how you stood on tippy-toes in the five-and-dime

store, craving a two-layer pencil box filled with erasers and new pencils and a protractor.

2. Make your fridge an art gallery and ask for new additions of artwork for your collection every six months or so. Along with photos, these precious reminders of your grandchild's ever-evolving interests and skills will give you the chance to remember them many times a day. You could even collect the art for each one and review their "portfolios" with them.

3. Take children to museums. Many museums offer children's tours and art activities related to their specialties. Art museums, museums of natural history, and museums focusing on other subject matter often have child-specific activities. Older children can enjoy virtual tours online instead of or in addition to live ones in the gallery.

4. Books about artists are often fascinating, even to young children. Lydia loves her Frida Kahlo books.

5. After-school and summer enrichment classes can supplement art instruction in schools. Grandparent Camp (see chapter 37) could include a trip to a local arts center for classes, resulting in a breather for the grandparents and artwork the grandchildren can proudly show their parents.

A CLUB IN THE HAND

Marilyn

It's not how big you are. It's how big you play.
—John Wooden

Stephen had done a lot of cute and surprising things in his almost three years among us, but this was beyond cute—and more than surprising. I was astonished. As his parents and I stood in their backyard, we were prepared to enjoy the spectacle of a tiny boy swinging his tiny golf club. We weren't fully prepared to see an inexplicable skill that took us all aback: he picked up the club and we saw him swing and hit, then swing and hit again, and again, and then again with perfect accuracy. His swing was sure and strong. He was in a zone.

Stephen is, as we've observed to each other on repeated occasions, a natural athlete. He's comfortable in his body, and he handles bats, balls, rackets, and anything with wheels as though they have been designed for his personal use. It's strange to use the term *authority* to describe anything a three-year-old does, but my impression that day, and on many occasions since, has been that when he has a ball in his hands or a bow or a paddle, he acts with authority. His eye-hand coordination is one of his more conspicuous gifts.

I say this not by way of exercising my bragging rights as a proud grandma (though I admit those rights are not lost on me) but because Stephen's remarkable capabilities—and later his brother's and his various cousins'—have led me to consider what we mean when we talk about children's gifts. The term *gifted*, as in "gifted and talented" programs in schools, can become one more unfortunate signpost that separates the "special" children from the not-so-special. The effect can, unfortunately, be that children who have already accrued privileges in life—privileges frequently connected to race and class—receive even more benefits. I also recognize the opposite danger of a false egalitarianism that flattens out helpful distinctions and useful, earned recognitions of achievement and skill.

Still, all children's gifts need to be cherished and fostered, and I think they deserve to be approached first of all with gratitude and awe. Unlearned aptitudes may be inscribed in DNA, but there's room for recognizing mystery in them as well. Something in them comes to us already honed and shaped. A gift is a kind of intuitive knowing—to be developed, certainly, but also to be allowed its own scope.

Maria Montessori offered the rule of thumb that adults should not, except in situations of danger, stop a child from doing what she thinks she can do. I imagine most of us can remember moments in parenting small children when we witnessed something like a quantum leap: they couldn't do it . . . then suddenly they could! One of my daughters wandered into the kitchen at a very early age, sat down with a little book, and proceeded to read to me—actually reading the words on the pages of a book she had not memorized or even read more than once. Something had clicked. This happens in language acquisition, as I had noticed in my own earlier years; after a couple of years of classroom German, I woke up in Austria one morning able to speak German without thinking in English. It just happened. That shift. That click. That moment when the kaleidoscope turns and the design changes altogether. To see those shifts happen in grandchildren, whose lives we witness from a new distance, is to come to new terms with a deep and mysterious dimension of what we call growth.

I've often thought about how Luke sums up the entirety of Jesus's childhood between the manger and his trip to Jerusalem at age twelve with the cryptic note that the child "increased in wisdom and in years, and in divine and human favor" (Luke 2:52). He "grew in grace," as some paraphrase that very brief record. Even when it is very small, the body is a repository of wisdom and grace, capable of growth, but given, in full—a gift. When we watch a little "natural athlete," we see one form of that wisdom at work. He knows what to do—before he can speak about it, before he knows the name of the strokes or of his own body parts. When we see wisdom at work, the first right response, I think, is reverence.

If we see a gift in those we've been given to love and help grow in grace, our job is to cherish that gift, but not by the lavish praise that can kill innocence with premature self-awareness. Rather, our job is to equip children with what they need to grow in that grace of body or mind, hand or eye, and bring the gift forth, eventually in the service of others. This is where our literal gifts to them—the balls, the drawing paper, the clay, the instruments, the lessons—can help theirs flower.

Suggestions for Grandparents

1. A good gift expresses both encouragement and hope. A baseball bat, swim goggles, a color-coded music score, colorful cooking or garden implements (the latter not necessarily from the children's department, if you can find small versions of the "real" thing): these things can let a child know you've noticed what they can do, believe they can become better at it, and want to help equip them to do that.

2. When a child is gifted, it's good to notice without over-praising. Montessori's wisdom—that focus on the child generally detracts from the child's own focus on the deep pleasure of exercising a skill—is helpful here. Rather than saying, "That was great!" you could notice and comment on the angle or force of the ball, the posture of the little dancer's feet, or the fact that all the lumps are gone from the batter.

PLEASURE IN LITTLE THINGS

Shirley

[To the mystic] grass is really a forest and the grass-hopper a dragon. Little things please great minds.
—G. K. Chesterton,
"The Puritan and the Anglican"

When little Lydia, at two and a half, visited our house, she spent the first few minutes walking from room to room and noticing things she remembered from her last visit nearly a year ago. She exclaimed gleefully when she spotted two Russian dolls and a family of brass llamas (the Llama Llama book series is one of her favorites) on the living room shelf. Outside, she asked to swing in the yellow seat and to lie down in the red-and-green striped hammock.

"The basement!" is Lydia's favorite place at our house. She goes to the door a dozen times a day, pausing to look up at the cow image on the Silver Summit Dairy sign, one her great-grandmother designed, as she carefully navigates the steps. Upon turning the corner to the area filled with garage-sale toys, she squeals with delight. "I ride the horsie. You sit on the blue ball," she commands.

In this space, everything pleases Lydia. Like Adam in the garden of Eden, she loves naming things. And counting. And singing. Color, especially the color purple, delights her. She never fails to praise it, and when she sees my royal purple velour robe, she claps her hands and pronounces it "special purple!"

Lydia loves machines that make noise—mixers, vacuums, hair dryers—but she doesn't want to get too close to them or even turn them on. She looks at them from a distance. In contrast, she crouches to examine twigs, pine cones, acorns, leaves, and spiderwebs. When we water the purple mums, she has to pull one off to examine it in the palm of her hand.

When she loves people or things, she never contents herself with saying their names just once. Soon I was hearing, "Grandma, Grandma, Grandma, come play with me in the basement."

And so I do. I play more in three days than I have for months.

Sometimes I am bored. Lydia has a high tolerance for repetition, whereas I am accustomed to seeking novelty. For her, gazing upon a thing of beauty—or bouncing on it or cutting paper with it or pasting it—gives her as much joy the tenth time as the first.

As Lydia and her parents pull out of our driveway on their journey back home, the morning sun illuminates the dew-laden grass of our front yard. I look closer to see a dandelion in its seed stage, covered with translucent water droplets, shining like the sun behind it. I so want Lydia to see this beautiful sight, but she has just disappeared down the road. Instead of taking her hand and asking her what she sees in the grass, I take a photo to share with her later.

I saw the dandelion in the first place because I was looking under my "boot-soles," something Walt Whitman instructed us to do long ago. Toddlers and poets often teach us the same things.

Suggestions for Grandparents

1. Do you have a grassy yard? An arboretum close by? A pumpkin patch or corn maze? You don't need more than a few square yards of flowers, grass, or even weeds to entertain a toddler. Keep asking, "What else do you see?"

2. Let your grandchild take the lead when you go on a walk. Observe how pleasurable apparently purposeless activity can be. All animals need such play. The human adult tends to forget this truth.

3. Walt Whitman's *Leaves of Grass* is a great book to read before, during, or after a grandchild visit. I look forward to reading Whitman *with* a grandchild someday. Until then, many of his trademark lines can fascinate a child. "I sing the body electric," "barbaric yawp," and "look for me under your boot-soles" are just three of many possible phrases that could prompt imitation, conversation, and playacting.

20

GOD'S FIRE TRUCK

Marilyn

These are the things I learned (in Kindergarten):
1. Share everything . . .

—Robert Fulghum

Stephen attended a Baptist preschool program the summer he was four. One day the teacher explained, after a playground squabble, that everything belonged to God. When his mother picked him up, Stephen ran out to greet her, tugged on her hand, and urged, "Come see God's fire truck!"

I loved that story and have told it to many friends, still moved as I tell it by the quality of innocence it contains. We so hope to protect that innocence in the very young until they have to face more complicated moral decisions. We need their innocence as much as they do. We need to be reminded, for instance, that all those material goods we consider "mine" ultimately belong to God—the shiny red metals, the whirring wheels, the sirens, the very molecules.

I thought of Stephen recently when I heard a talk by a young economist who posed the deceptively simple question, "How does a thing become property?" It's not just an economic question, or a political one; it is philosophical and theological and quite personal. Children's playground disputes over property rights are important formative moments. How we intervene in children's arguments over material stuff—or choose not to—has lasting effects.

Our interventions in our grandchildren's squabbles are intermittent, and they may be at odds with parents whose methods of adjudicating those disputes are either more laissez-faire or more legalistic than our own. As grandchildren have come along, we've found that it's good to acknowledge those differences, make honest efforts to honor their parents' wishes, and also affirm some intrafamilial diversity: Grandma's house, Grandma's rules. (No, the irony is not lost on me: invoking property rights may seem out of keeping with the point at hand!) Who gets what, when, and on what terms are questions that will be revisited for a long time to come. And God may or may not be invoked as we try to distribute clay or pool toys. But the deep truth that "it's all God's stuff" is not a bad reminder, particularly when we think about much larger questions of distribution of wealth.

Having said that, when God does enter into the conversation, we may need to tread more carefully. Our adult children's families might maintain differing relationships to faith and faith communities, prayer, Scripture, religious holidays, and worship services. We try not to preach or proselytize in the delicate teaching moments we're given with the children who, thus far, trust our guidance. It's a good challenge to find simple, clear language and accessible analogies for complicated matters: why another child with an invisible disability might need special privileges, why we might suspend rules about whose turn it is when a sibling is just having a very sad day, why whining doesn't—and shouldn't—work. Sometimes those explanations lend themselves very easily to the creation story or parables or a beatitude. More often, the moment simply calls for a little education in ambiguity: "fair" can't be reduced to a hard and fast rule; "deserves" is a word that leads to deep places; "mine" . . . well . . . isn't, exactly.

We were quite delighted when, a few months after the revelation of God's fire truck, we came home to hear Stephen's piping little voice on our voice mail. Without a word of greeting, he recited boldly, "Rejoice in the Lord always! Again I say, rejoice! Philippians 4:4" (with a particularly careful emphasis on *Philippians*). I imagine he learned those words, his first memorized Bible verse, at the same Baptist preschool. It's a good one to start with and to return to after all disputes over property, or whose turn it is, or who gets to play what music in the car.

There's a place of joy we can get to if we follow the guidance we've been given, and we can show our grandchildren the way there. Letting them see us rejoice, and notice what makes us rejoice, can help them do likewise—even, perhaps, when someone else happens to be ringing the bell on God's fire truck.

Suggestions for Grandparents

1. Sharing has a strong learning curve. Some would say our culture complicates it with too much emphasis on competition. One way to encourage it is to have a box of toys for children's visits that's specifically the "sharing box." Things in there are to be distributed or time-shared. You might come up with a particular incentive for the child who gets to be the distributor or timekeeper that day.

2. It's a good discipline to notice our own language of possession. We can practice speaking about what is given, what has been given to us, who else made the things we enjoy, how many hands helped make them. That way, our grandchildren's—and our own—notion of what is "mine" is gradually modified by an awareness of how many others have some claim on an item or credit for it. A good website to take children to when they're old enough is The Story of Stuff (https://www.storyofstuff.org/movies/story -of-stuff/). The simple stick-figure cartoons can be helpful in introducing children to where stuff comes from and where it goes.

21

MEETINGS WITH TREES

Marilyn

I walk slowly and bow often.
  —Mary Oliver, "When I Walk through the Trees"

When Benjamin was two, he began visiting trees. On walks around the neighborhood, he would suddenly let go of my hand and, with great deliberation, head for a particular tree, put his arms around it as far as they could reach, rest his head against the bark, and stand there for a few moments. He had an unusually rich vocabulary for a two-year-old thanks to his articulate parents, but he offered no explanation for this behavior. After apparently communing with the tree for a minute or so, he'd return to my side and take my hand, and we'd continue our walk.

I was intrigued—even moved. As climate change, defor-
estation, and species extinction become more evident, I have
become increasingly conscious of the vulnerability of the living beings around us. Dry leaves, dry grasses, wildfires, and
signs in public bathrooms urging us to conserve water offer
daily reminders of drought in my state; in others, flooding
presents a real and recurrent danger. I wonder how children
are internalizing that awareness. Benjamin hadn't yet begun
school, but since those early excursions, he has learned
something about the life of plants and why certain species of
plants and animals need protection. It may be that in those
early days, he was responding to something in trees that had
little directly to do with their vulnerability or thirst. What did
seem clear was that his interest in trees was relational.

On one memorable walk, he asked me, as we passed by a
large cedar tree, "Amma, what is the tree doing?" It seemed
a question to take seriously and to answer with care. I loved
the implied assumption that trees weren't just standing there
but that they were doing something. He seemed to think they
were going about their business—maybe their Father's business, as the young Jesus suggested he was doing in Luke 2.
And Benjamin wanted to mind that business.

"Trees do a lot of things," I said, and as he seemed to want
details, I offered as simple a science lesson as I could devise
while we stood in the shade of the cedar: "They take in sunlight and water and food from the soil and make them into
wood and leaves the way you make your food into bones
and muscles. And when they breathe in, they take in a kind
of air called carbon dioxide. When they breathe out, they
make oxygen for us to breathe. We need oxygen to live. When
we breathe in, we receive the oxygen they make. When we

breathe out, we breathe out the carbon dioxide they need to live. Pretty great how that works, isn't it? Every time we breathe in and out, we're exchanging gifts with the trees."

Benjamin listened without comment. We continued our walk, finding pine cones and acorns, pausing to look both ways before we crossed the street, chatting about what was for dinner. On our way home, as we came to the cedar tree, he tugged at my hand and stopped. Wordlessly, he took in a deep breath and exhaled forcibly. Then another, and another. It seemed he was giving the tree a little extra hit of carbon dioxide. It seemed a remarkable act of recognition and thanksgiving. The cedar got a few extra hugs that season. It was his learning tree.

Besides classics like *The Giving Tree* and *The Lorax*, dozens of children's books now feature trees as beings whose lives are entwined with ours in deep and intimate ways. I'm grateful for every one of the dozens of stories, songs, and poems that remind them and us that plant life matters—including the blessing of plant life in Genesis and Isaiah's promise that all the trees will clap their hands. I hope one day to give Benjamin a copy of *The Green Bible*, in which passages that have to do with the earth and its creatures are printed in green. Foregrounding that dimension of a sacred story makes it harder to consign other living beings to the lifeless status of "resources."

On his weekly visits, Benjamin often heads out to the backyard, where he inspects the lime tree he requested for his birthday (and for which we are providing foster care until he finds time and space and parental help to take it home). He waters various potted herbs. Sometimes we head to the nursery to pick out a few more. I have to deal with my guilt when, due to my own travel or distraction, one of his beloved plants languishes or dies between visits. I've been known to sneak in substitute seedlings. He notices.

Whatever I can do to encourage his tender interest in plant life, and in life processes, seems important, not only because of his unusual attunement to plants but because of the timeliness of that sensitivity. Someday Benjamin may be able to contribute to conversations we all need to be having about rainforests and species preservation and resilience. Benjamin has inspired me to continue my own learning; I can't wait to share with him William Bryant Logan's lovely books *Dirt* and *Oak* and *Air* (distinguished, among other things, by their catchy titles) and Wendell Berry's essays.

Benjamin has helped me leave my computer long enough to learn the names of the plants in our small but nicely varied yard—ginkgo and pistache and dogwood and maple, crepe myrtle and guava and jasmine. The roll call itself is a pleasure. When our little Adam comes inside covered in potting soil or summons me out to see a new bug, my heart is lifted up. He's a witness. It's a calling.

Suggestions for Grandparents

1. Visit your plant neighbors! You could look up three interesting things to know about this tree (or plant) and write them out on small cards. These can be laminated and attached to ice cream sticks to be placed near the plant, or they could be kept in a "garden guide" on a coffee table for visitors. One or another grandchild might love the role of garden guide.

2. Make watering plants an occasion for conversation rather than a chore. Talking to the plants—using personal

pronouns if you're so inclined—doesn't have to "Disneyfy" them. On the contrary, it can help open up reflection at any age on what the poet Dylan Thomas called "the force that through the green fuse drives the flower."

3. A number of good documentaries about plants and trees are available to watch with kids: *The Secret World of Trees*, *The Secret World of Plants*, *In the Mind of Plants*, and *What Plants Talk About* are just a few that can help viewers of any age see plants' lives—and their own—in new terms.

EVERY LIVING THING

Marilyn

Time in nature is not leisure time; it's an essential investment in our children's health (and also, by the way, in our own).
                    —Richard Louv, *Last Child in the Woods*

Our suburban grandchildren have spent a lot of time on playground equipment in local parks, making castles and tunnels on beaches, and running in the grass with lumbering, benevolent dogs. Occasionally their parents have packed all the necessary equipment and taken them tent camping in the nearby Sierras. When they visit, we putter around in the backyard, inspecting bugs and picking fruit when it's available on several productive trees. Two of them go to a school where a flourishing garden is part of the curriculum. One learned to wield a spade and harvest cauliflower when he was five, giving him a skill set and a source of pleasure.

But by historical standards, their outdoor life is pretty minimal and likely to be reduced as time goes on and more and more of their day is spent online and in classrooms. I began to think about their relationship to nature, and my own, in new ways when I read Richard Louv's beautiful and disturbing book *Last Child in the Woods: Saving Our Children from Nature-Deficit Disorder*. In it, he cites studies that confirm what common sense probably suggests: that children thrive emotionally, concentrate better, and actually heal from physical ailments or injuries more quickly in the presence of other living, growing beings—not just people and pets, but trees and grass and dirt and bugs and lizards and weeds. Some of the research involved putting plants in classrooms and measuring children's sustained focus. Others measured rates of healing when plants were placed in hospital rooms.

Even babies in this generation are spending more time indoors or constrained in car seats than babies in previous eras. Many are breathing indoor air (a problem in more homes than we'd like to think) or being walked around in shopping malls or on city streets more than being taken to natural outdoor spaces. Jane Clark, a University of Maryland professor of kinesiology, calls them "containerized kids" because of the hours they spend in car seats, strollers, high chairs, and gated rooms. In the name of protection—a concern ratcheted up by the 2020 pandemic—fewer of the largely urbanized young are being formed by an intimate connection with the natural world.

Most of us can't retrieve life on the farm or the freedom of our own childhoods for our grandchildren. Our memories from childhood may include ball games in vacant city lots, climbing trees in uncultivated open spaces, exploring river-banks, or being in close proximity to what was truly wild. As we incline toward more insistent standards of personal pro-tection, we collectively deprive kids of something Richard Louv and others insist they need for spiritual, emotional, and physical growth.

As we care for kids in the world they have now, parents and grandparents are at a learning edge: keeping them safe entails avoiding a host of new dangers, some of which are out of our control. And giving them contact with the soil, the sun, the snow, and crashing waves or storms or swiftly flowing streams is harder as development encroaches upon wild spaces and regulates access. Keeping them safe, Louv and others would argue, has to involve, paradoxically, letting them take some risks—touching things that are "unsanitary," picking up worms, pricking their fingers on thorns, and drag-ging in pockets full of rocks and twigs. How can parents and grandparents find the right balance, not just in terms of what they're allowed to do but also when deciding between pro-tecting children and letting them try things? Between keep-ing them safe and letting them explore the natural world on their own? And what are the trade-offs?

Plenty of studies testify to the consequences of nature deprivation, which generally include diminished physical exercise but also diminished resilience, creativity, and curi-osity. We can offset some of the losses urban life entails by making sure kids have plants indoors as well as outdoors, or at least on balconies, and that they are involved in watering those plants, noticing when new leaves appear, and adding plant food. We can make sure there are animals in their lives—if not at their homes, perhaps at ours. Perhaps we can help them get to know neighborhood pets. We can point out small creatures and talk about how they live—ants on the bark of a tree, or bees hovering around a flower, or the occasional harmless spider making its unwelcome way up the wall of the bathroom. We can work against the impulse to treat the occasional line of ants on the sink only as pests and talk first about why they're there and what they do with their tiny, busy lives.

Learning the names of other creatures puts us in relationship with them, and it's a great way to keep both us and the grandchildren we love connected to the creatures around us who are innocent, tolerant, steady, and quite literally lifegiving. Knowing that the tree in the yard is a maple or mulberry, that the bush over there is a forsythia, that deer like to eat the hydrangeas, that bees like cosmos—this is useful knowledge, to be sure. This knowledge makes us all more attentive to the ways we are connected to them through our senses and through the air we exchange. This knowledge must also be relearned—sometimes from scientists and sometimes from children—when we let them lead us into the woods.

Suggestions for Grandparents

1. Find out what local parks and recreation department staff know about safe outdoor spaces beyond parks, what pesticides are being used locally, what insects and small

creatures are safe, and which to watch out for. Learn about spiders—most are harmless.

2. Have a small tree or plant your grandchild can help care for when he or she visits and include some conversation about it in each visit. You can do the same with pets: if you have one, engage small children not only in playing with it but also in talking about what it needs, what it knows, and why it behaves as it does.

3. There are plenty of good books about gardens, insects, and the outdoors for young children. A couple of good examples are Tim McCanna's *In a Garden*, illustrated by Aimée Sicuro, and *Up in the Garden and Down in the Dirt* by Kate Messner and Christopher Silas Neal (one of the Over and Under series—four books about life above the earth's surface and beneath the soil and water).

4. Make a terrarium. Easy instructions are readily available on YouTube.

23

LIFELONG LEARNING

Marilyn

The adventure of life is to learn.
—William Arthur Ward

I recently downloaded a plant identification app. Now I know that the impressive tree down the street is a camphor tree and that the flowering bush I was wondering about is a crepe myrtle. Benjamin and Hannah and I have taken "plant walks" in their neighborhood to see how many we could name. When we've finished in their neighborhood and ours, we'll head down to the river and see what new names we can add to the list.

Botany is an interest for me but an area in which I could use a lot more education. I also don't know much about dog training and canine intelligence, but all our grandchildren are growing up with dogs, and I'm getting a chance to learn as I get to know their doggy ways. Reading children's books in Spanish to support one daughter-in-law's efforts to give her California baby an early start at being bilingual helps me reclaim the Spanish I studied in college: maybe I can make it usable again. As each baby has approached pre-school age, the books I read years ago about developmental psychology and early childhood education have seemed worth revisiting. My ongoing concerns about the chemicals and food additives we are living with have been heightened; I'm motivated to do a little more homework and become a little more active in protecting them and all children from pesticides and dubious preservatives.

So when I say to friends that I'm "learning a lot" by being a grandmother, I mean more than learning how to love and care for this particular child. Each grandchild opens doors to new education, reeducation, and continuing education. Colleges and universities offer courses for adults, from newly minted graduates to elders, that usually invoke the ideal of "lifelong learning." Our local university hosts a program called "Renaissance" every Friday, where older adults offer and take free classes. I applaud these efforts. If I ran the zoo, we'd all be "in school" one day a week for the rest of our lives. And as I have found, a day a week with grandchildren can be a pretty good program in continuing education.

The fun of learning with them begins with the practice of hearing their apparently random questions—What does that little wire do? What made the hummingbird stop right there?—as invitations to find out. We can, of course, find answers to almost anything online using a search engine, but we can also postpone that easy route long enough to peer at the thing in question, speculate out loud, imagine, maybe find pictures in a book, and invite the little questioner to do the same. It's a rich process that's too easily foreshortened by easy internet access. Learning isn't just taking the shortest route to answers—sometimes it means playing with the question for a while.

"Live the questions," Rilke wrote. "Live your way into the answer." Even the answer to a specific question like the name of a tree, if we live the question for a while, might get us to a fun conversation about naming trees, about how we get our names, about what one writer called "the hidden life of trees"—and perhaps about the hidden life of a child who is, from the very beginning, a mystery and a marvel.

Suggestions for Grandparents

1. "Let's find out" can become a game with variations, depending on the age of the child. Let's find out three things about radishes . . . or what roads are made of. Let's find out what two other people know about this. Let's find out how much we can find out when we pick it up, turn it over, watch what it does in the dirt, and look at it with a magnifying glass.

2. Cooking together offers a wide range of learning moments: What do you think happens to the flour when you stir it in? Why do you think the cookies spread out in the oven? What might happen if you put too much water in? Those conversations make plenty of room for imagination and story as well as instruction.

3. Walks and well-illustrated books provide the tactile experiences children often miss if they rush too quickly to
   online answers. Many of us are in a position to take time
   with both in ways that are harder for busy parents. A conversation with those parents might produce a useful list of
   learning activities children can do at your house that they
   don't tend to do or can't do at home.

WHO THEY ARE, WHERE THEY ARE

Marilyn

Where you are is who you are.

—Frances Mayes

When I was in fourth grade, all children in California public schools were taught a rather selective version of California history before being taught a similarly selective version of US history, which was then standard fifth-grade fare. We made salt and flour topo maps of our long state with its two bumpy mountain ranges, marking Lake Tahoe with a thumbprint and scooping out little indentations for the

WHO THEY ARE, WHERE THEY ARE

San Francisco and Monterey Bays. We were also taught about Father Junípero Serra's long journey up the coast, and we were taken on field trips to the nearest of the twenty-one Catholic missions he founded. We trekked around Yosemite, learning the names of wild flora, looking (mostly in vain) for bears, and learning about the life of John Muir. I thought all kids were learning what we were learning. It didn't occur to me until later that kids growing up in Kansas or Iowa might be learning a very different kind of natural history, and kids in Massachusetts or South Carolina might be hearing a slightly different repertoire of stories about the American past.

How will our California grandchildren be taught? Certainly what they learn will have a lot to do with where they learn it. At the preschool little Chris attends, a big garden flourishes in months when children in upstate New York are pulling on boots and gathering autumn leaves. Chris has his own watering can and knows which weeds to pull up. After gardening, he loves to jump in the pool, even though, by California standards, October is getting downright chilly. He's been to Yosemite and seen Half Dome but hasn't been to the Badlands or Lake Michigan. He's never seen a bayou.

One answer to how and what our grandchildren will learn is that they will begin where they are. And what they see will shape their imaginations, their sense of space and time, and their relationships to rivers, forests, and city parks.

If we live far away from our grandchildren, we can help furnish their widening imaginations with stories from elsewhere and eventually, perhaps, with summer trips. But it's good to take stock of what they see and hear and navigate. Their natural and built environments may be different—and their sense of what's "normal"—and their sociological land-scapes may be different as well.

Since 2014, Latinos have outnumbered those who iden-tify as white in California. "White" northern European immigrants were preceded here, of course, not only by well-established Indigenous peoples but also by Hispanic and Mexican residents. It *was* Mexico. It is not unusual for a classroom in California cities and most suburbs to include children from several racial and ethnic ancestries—Chinese, Vietnamese, Hmong, Central American, Indian, Polynesian, among others. I recently read that more than ninety-two lan-guages are represented in LA County schools. As kids grow up in those schools, they will, given the larger cultural his-tory and climate, very likely witness tensions arising around the differences. But they're just as likely to take some of those differences for granted and to have best friends from fami-lies that differ from their own in race, religion, eating pat-terns, notions of parental authority, and primary language. Kids growing up in far more homogenous environments will discover much of the same richness and run into similar ten-sions in the wider world as they venture outward, but their grounding points, their notions of normal, and their sense of what friendship requires will be different.

We will have a lot to do with how Chris learns about flora and fauna, how he learns (and relearns) American history, how he learns to love the earth and its people, and how he develops and later revises his sense of place, including boundaries and what they're about. That adventure may lie outside of and beyond those boundaries—including local, regional, and national loyalties. Also including the fact that some places are far more sheltered and privileged and comfortable than others.

We can take our grandchildren to new places in books, sometimes in movies, sometimes in cars and planes. My hope is that each of our growing gaggle of grandchildren will become citizens of the earth and be able to enjoy some of its rich diversity. I hope they recognize home as the place you start from, learn from, and perhaps love, but only the beginning of a widening stage on which their stories may be played out in many acts, among many actors, all of whom are on their own journeys of discovery.

Suggestions for Grandparents

1. One way of exploring where small children are is to take them on "sense walks"—a "smell walk," a "sound walk," a "touch/texture walk"—during which you pause over different noticings. Another is to collect and label things, perhaps in a "museum box" that can be filled with leaves, feathers, stones, and—if you're willing—an occasional dead bug.

2. Mapping can begin early, and maps become an ongoing matter of interest, especially if children are introduced to different kinds—not just those that show political boundaries or roads but topographical maps, maps of water systems, maps of houses' plumbing systems, maps that show where different people groups come from. One way to start is by drawing little maps with children, showing them how to represent a few landmarks that lie between here and the grocery store (or between home and Grandma's house).

3. A wide range of children's books address questions on topics of race, class, gender, and other differences to small children and focus on justice in ways children can readily grasp. A few of these worth checking out are *Sulwe* by Lupita Nyong'o, *Fry Bread: A Native American Family Story* by Kevin Noble Maillard, and *All Are Welcome* by Alexandra Penfold and Suzanne Kaufman. And, of course, dolls and toys that represent a range of races and ethnicities can help both normalize differences and spark conversations about them.

4. Some schools and teachers are open to grandparents as guest speakers. If you are a visitor from a different and interesting place, you might volunteer to go tell about your place.

WHAT GOOD GRANDPARENTS DO

Marilyn

Learn about their techno-toys
And limit them
Trust their capacity for complexity
Model respectful behavior
And require it
Take them seriously
Laugh at their riddles
Invent ways to make veggies inviting
Keep a magnifying glass handy
Make space for bug specimens

Equip them for hard things
Watch what they see on screens
And talk with them about it
Avoid overpraising
And overspending
Wonder with them
Help them craft good questions
Simplify without dumbing down
Get clear about boundaries
And tell them why
Help them get to know trees by name
Help them notice
Give them historical perspective
Be wholly present

Suggestions for Grandparents

1. This chapter, chapter 15, and chapter 43 are lists. You may find that lists help you sort through complex ideas, or notice things you had not seen previously, or illustrate lavish abundance. Plus they are fun! Choose a subject, make a list, and put it up on the fridge. Let other people add to it.

2. Encourage your grandchild to make a list. Kids love to make Christmas and birthday gift lists. You can start there and then branch out: Things that make me happy. Gifts I would like to give. The names of all the pets on our street. Names of all the flowers in our garden.

PART III
FEELINGS

But feelings can't be ignored, no matter how unjust or ungrateful they seem.

—Anne Frank, *The Diary of a Young Girl*

26

ON NOT BEING BRAVE

Marilyn

A child's fear is a world whose dark corners are quite unknown to grownup people.

—Julien Green

I was spending the night with Benjamin and Hannah while their parents took a much-needed overnight break. I knew Benjamin had been waking with nighttime fears, so I took some extra time with him before bed, reading, assuring him that I was nearby and that his parents would be home in the morning, and tucking him in. His little sister, not inclined to anxiety, sailed through the bedtime rituals and went giggling to bed with her bunny.

Unsurprisingly, after a couple of hours, Benjamin was awake and afraid. I held him. We talked about nighttime, about all the creatures who come out at night—owls, foxes, and, way up in the mountains, mother bears—looking not for people but for food for their babies. We talked about how cozy it is to be tucked in, to lie quietly if you can't sleep and look at stars or listen for nighttime sounds.

He listened and calmed down a bit, but then he began to cry again. When I asked what was wrong, he said, "I'm supposed to take care of Hannah because I'm her big brother." Clearly, he felt he was falling down on the job. He didn't know it wasn't his job.

How easy it is, I realized, for children to misinterpret what are meant to be simple encouragements. I could just hear his folks saying, "Take good care of your little sister" as a way of encouraging him to take pride in his big-brother role—not, I'm sure, to inflict a daunting responsibility on a four-year-old.

Benjamin was in a quandary. He was supposed to be brave and protective, but he felt afraid and, perhaps, unprotected as he lay awake in the dark, even though he knew a loving adult was just steps away.

His parents and I all addressed the misunderstanding within a day. We assured him that the grown-ups were responsible for Hannah and that he didn't have to take care of her. Being a good big brother just meant being kind and funny and, say, not grabbing her toys when she made him mad. We assured him that the doors were locked at night and that his parents took every care for his safety.

Most importantly, I think, we told him he didn't have to be brave. Permission to be afraid is important. Even small children know bad things do happen to people. I remember how unhelpful it was when my lovely, deeply faithful mother responded to my own nighttime fears by saying not to be afraid—just pray and know that God would take care of me. I believe in prayer, and in loving, divine presence and guidance. But at that moment, standing in our kitchen in my flannel pajamas, I needed permission to be afraid. I needed her to say, "Oh, I know—sometimes things are scarier at night. Tell me about what's scary."

Invoking faith or bravery in the moment of fear can be counterproductive for a child. I've come to believe that the very best first response to fear is to hold them and listen. And listen some more before jumping in to comfort or reassure. "Tell me what you're afraid of. . . . Is there more? . . . What's the scariest part?" can, paradoxically, be empowering. As a child opens up into telling his experience, he assumes a kind of authority over it, and that goes a long way toward restoring perspective and confidence.

Some time ago, I heard a bit of simple wisdom that has helped me through many unsettling encounters with children. Whatever anxieties small children bring to you, there are two things they really want to know: "Do you love me?" and "Who's in charge?" The answer is always important and always the same. Yes, I love you. And I'm in charge. (And in the right context, God is in charge. But that may come later.)

Think about how much lighter you feel now and then when another adult, perhaps a spouse, simply says, "Don't worry, honey. I'll take care of it." The burden of responsibility shifts and the energy that might have leaked into a pool of anxiety comes back to you, available for better purposes.

There's plenty to be afraid of. Our grandchildren are growing up in a climate of pervasive, chronic challenges our generation didn't have to face. We'll need to help equip them along the way to face fear with honesty, with trust in a beloved community, and, yes, with courage. It will be a gradual process, probably involving a lot of nighttime moments and ritual reassurances. Ritual reassurances implant messages that may last a lifetime. A ninety-eight-year-old man once told me he had recited the little prayer his mother taught him every night of his life. Indeed, as we learn to be elders and guides, we will need to address our own fears and foster our own deepest sources of faith and wisdom.

In the meantime, while they are small and vulnerable, it can help to tell them these simple truths while they are wrapped in our arms near the night-light: I love you. Your parents love you. God who made you loves you. We're in charge. You don't have to be. You don't even have to be brave. It's OK to be afraid. But for tonight, right now, you can take some deep breaths and relax into delicious sleep. I'll be right nearby.

Suggestions for Grandparents

1. A few classic bedtime books provide lasting gentle messages in addition to those that come naturally in the course of conversation. Well worth having in your library are *Goodnight Moon* by Margaret Wise Brown, of course, and *Little Owl's Night* by Divya Srinivasan, and *The Owl Who Was Afraid of the Dark* by Jill Tomlinson. Another book, which offers healthy permission to be afraid and encouragement that there's a way through fear, is Cornelia Maude Spelman's *When I Feel Scared*.

2. Songs can supplement stories as ways of instilling peace and confidence. In addition to standard lullabies, a few lovely songs from popular artists and groups that offer a sense of safety for the night are John Lennon's "Beautiful Boy" (easily adapted for our beautiful girls!), Bob Marley's "Three Little Birds," and Bill Withers's "Lean on Me."

3. You can find a lovely range of soothing instrumental music for relaxation, some of it focused especially on young listeners, online. See, for example, https://www.youtube.com/watch?v=qFZKK7K52uQ.

4. For families who share faith, moments of fear are a good time to introduce, without "shoulds," faith language that can plant roots of lasting trust. One example is a simple verse from Scripture like Psalm 4:8 NIV: "In peace I will lie down and sleep, for you alone, Lord, make me dwell in safety."

27

MR. ROGERS'S SECRET

Shirley

The world is not always a kind place. That's something all children learn for themselves, whether we want them to or not, but it's something they really need our help to understand.

—Fred Rogers

Toddler Lydia is starting to recognize when she needs to go potty—often when it's a bit too late. To encourage her interest, I take her to the potty any time she makes the announcement. Just as I am about to put her on the seat, she says with a big smile, "Stop!" Then she adds, "When you have to go potty, stop! . . . and go right away."

"Is that what Daniel Tiger does?" I ask.

"Yes."

She reaches for the handle behind her and sings, "Flush and wash and be on your way." Then she jumps up on the stool in front of the sink and cheerfully washes her little paws.

I am certain that soon Lydia will handle the potty accurately and instinctively, the way Serena Williams smashes a backhand. Until then, she has lots of steps to learn. The first one is "stop!"

The teacher behind the potty song, Fred Rogers, pioneered a new kind of children's television on PBS through his beloved and long-running show *Mister Rogers' Neighborhood*. Though he died in 2003, his legacy keeps growing. The current animated PBS program *Daniel Tiger's Neighborhood*, available online and on-air, is reaching even more children than the original show, with fifty-one million streams in one month in 2019.

Mr. Rogers's genius consisted of knowing that children need a special kind of love. Long before "social and emotional learning" was a highly specialized field in child psychology, he knew that children need to learn self-regulation as toddlers. He knew that the best way to teach children was not to punish them or isolate them or ignore them (all popular parenting techniques in his day) but to teach them how to be powerful.

If you wet your pants, or if you throw a fit, or if you steal a toy, or if you dump your milk on the floor, you have the power to do something to change the unhappiness you and those around you are feeling. You can stop.

Toddlers walk around in a jungle of giants, seeing most people from the vantage point of their hips or knees. They often feel powerless. By age two, they want to address the power imbalance. Parents know they need to exert authority, but they don't want to be authoritarian. They seek advice from whatever the reigning orthodoxy on child-rearing happens to be among their friends and trusted sources.

We grandparents can reinforce what our adult children are trying to do and can talk to them about what we think is most helpful during a power struggle. In our own homes, we can make rules like "no hitting," or we can establish a "quiet corner" and ask if the child needs to go there.

When we are in the grandchild's home, stepping away while parents discipline is likely the best thing for us to do. And if the child attempts to evade parental boundaries by asking us as grandparents for help? We can say no to getting involved. We can avoid offering bribes or enticements as distractions as well; they only teach the child how to manipulate adult authority. You will probably break this rule once or twice. I have.

Mr. Rogers knew a great deal about anger. He had been bullied and lonely as a child, and he knew that stuffing down emotion without acknowledging it is not good. Instead of repressing feelings of rage, he wrote a song about them. The time for a child to learn the song, of course, is not in the heat of anger, but it can be very helpful to use the song to talk about feelings before they erupt and to reflect on what we can learn after an outburst.

Mr. Rogers's song is called "What Do You Do with the Mad That You Feel?" Instead of preaching, it asks a great question and then dramatizes it. No holds barred. (You can find the lyrics online.) The song gives children permission to feel angry and then to choose creative ways to express the anger in ways that don't harm others. The decision to stop—to refrain from harming another outburst of anger—is empowering.

A friend told a group of grandmas how her eight-year-old grandchild amazed her this past Christmas. When Sophie was in the midst of a tug-of-war with her cousin, she looked up and said, "It's a good thing no one else can know our thoughts!" Sophie was aware she was angry and just as aware that she had choices. She used that power to put a thought into words—almost like writing a song.

If we grandparents can make any contribution to a child's ability to stop at the right time, in the right way—if we can help them choose to replace a feeling of rage with a feeling of self-control—well, we will have given a gift much greater than a battery-powered toy BMW or even a topped-up 529 college savings account.

We elders can still learn this lesson ourselves. If we, too, struggle with self-regulation, rage, anxiety, guilt, or shame, it's never too late to stop. Or as my friend Susan used to say, "It's never too late to have a happy childhood."

Toward the end of his life, Fred Rogers received Emmys and honorary degrees and lifetime achievement awards. When receiving awards, he would almost always do the same thing. First, he would stop. Then he would say, "I'd like to give you all an invisible gift. A gift of a silent minute to think about those who have helped you become who you are today."

Thank you, Fred Rogers, for helping us become better grandparents.

Suggestions for Grandparents

1. In the last few years, Mr. Rogers has become even more of a folk hero than he was even in his much-honored lifetime. *A Beautiful Day in the Neighborhood* (2019), starring Tom Hanks, tells how Fred Rogers transformed the lives of adults as well as children. *Won't You Be My Neighbor?* (2018) is a powerful documentary about his life.

2. *You Are My Friend*, written by Aimee Reid and illustrated by Matt Phelan, is a delightful children's book about Fred Rogers. It tells the story of his childhood, which was full of illness and loneliness, and how he was supported by his parents. It offers a clue as to how he later was able to use puppets and songs to teach children what he himself had needed to learn.

3. *Daniel Tiger's Neighborhood* likely airs daily on a PBS station near you. There are also PBS Kids apps for computers, tablets, and phones. You can also find short online videos all about feelings, including "What Do You Do with the Mad That You Feel?"

A CANDLE IN THE DARKNESS

Shirley

Make of yourself a light.
—Mary Oliver, "The Buddha's Last Instructions"

"Sometimes all I can do is light a candle," Marilyn said.

Marilyn and I talked with each other every week for more than a year while we were writing this book. Chapters emerged from conversations as we shared responses to each other's words and opened up our lives to each other. Sometimes we didn't talk about our grandchildren at all.

During the pandemic, we could not visit our families in person. They could have used our help, as all of them were struggling to do work from home, childcare, and sometimes school from home. But our children knew we, as senior citizens, were especially vulnerable to the coronavirus. They became our protectors and occasional scolds if they thought we weren't being careful enough about social distancing or other pandemic guidelines.

Our familial roles were beginning to reverse. This reversal happens to most elderly people once a disability of any kind sets in. The children start to sound like parents, giving advice and instruction. We know that time will come if we are lucky enough to live long; we just didn't expect it to erupt in our late sixties and early seventies! After all, "sixty is the new forty," right?

The grandparenting season can be a respite from power struggles. We give up the power we had as parents. If we're lucky, our children accept our participation in their lives and maybe even welcome it. We hold ourselves in check when tempted to give advice. Or try to. Our children can correct us if we don't. At any rate, our mutual focus is on the child or children. We try to form a team.

But sometimes things go wrong. Our children suffer physically or emotionally, or both, during times of stress. They may share some of their pain with us. They may choose not to do so. We, at the other end of the phone or computer, must wait. We must wait until they're ready to talk or willing to unburden themselves to us.

We refuse, as parents, to be passive. So how do we wait actively?

Marilyn's idea of lighting a candle has helped me when I am waiting for updates from our adult children. As I go about my day, I notice the flickering flame, reminding me to breathe a silent prayer for peace, hope, wisdom, or joy. Often in the midst of passive suffering—an adult child's undiagnosed

symptoms, a grandchild's anxiety, or other complex realities I don't control—I call on my imagination. Staring at the
flame, I bring my child to mind and create a mental image:
of scientists squinting into microscopes, or pilgrims singing
as they walk, or mountain climbers linking up with ropes
and carabiners. Sitting with the candle, holding the image on
behalf of a family member, not only helps me deal with my
own anxiety and uncertainty; it also allows me to feel active
while sitting in my chair.

My friend Carolyn is an expert in trauma and resilience.
I described my feeling of helplessness at not being able
to go to my family during the pandemic. I told her about
the image I had created of our family being scientists in
white coats, opening the door of a laboratory, trying to crack
the code of a problem, preparing by breathing deeply
together. Then I said, "That's probably not helpful to anyone
but me right now."

Carolyn nodded and said, "Sometimes we just have to
send our love energetically."

Author and friend Parker J. Palmer, in his well-known book
Let Your Life Speak, describes a time during a sleepless night
when he heard a voice saying simply, "I love you, Parker." The
voice was a sign, coming from within him, of grace. At
the time, he could not accept freely given love because he
was sunk deep into self-hatred. But the sign left its mark.
He has never forgotten it or doubted its validity.

When we can't hug our children and grandchildren or go
to them, we can still light a candle. We can open our hearts
and pour out our prayers. We can listen to calming music.
We can take nuggets of whatever wisdom we have gained
and send notes, texts, emails. We can send whispers of love

to all our children and grandchildren on their sleepless nights—and ours.

By taking these kinds of actions, we calm our own hearts and minds, which are likely to be noisy places in the presence of a threat. During the pandemic, I took a virtual class on resilience offered by my friend Carolyn. She uses Emotional Freedom Techniques as a tool to reduce anxiety and increase the healing power of the body, mind, and spirit.

As I tapped the meridian points on my body, I used the images of exploration and of consolation—for example, the biblical image of the mother hen with her chicks. I acknowledged that I was feeling helpless while I loved and accepted myself.

Inside, I felt a tiny flicker. Out of that flicker can come surprises: Warmth that penetrates. A memory with staying power. A great conflagration of love.

The light we make for our dear ones is the light that comes from our own very being. Light a candle. Make of yourself a light.

Suggestions for Grandparents

1. The poetry of Mary Oliver, collected in the book *Devotions: The Selected Poems of Mary Oliver*, offers light for dark times.
2. Parker Palmer describes his descent into darkness, and his return from it, in *Let Your Life Speak: Listening for the Voice of Vocation*.
3. Carolyn Yoder's work on trauma and resilience can be accessed online. Search for "Peace after Trauma."

29

HARD TIMES

Marilyn

*If we are to reach real peace in this world . . . we shall
have to begin with children.*

—Mahatma Gandhi

I recently spoke with a sixteen-year-old about how his classmates were handling waves of world news that many find
overwhelming—climate change, economic instability, political conflict, and the coronavirus, for example. "Are kids
you know depressed?" I asked.

"Some are," he answered, "but for a lot of us, it's just the
world we live in. We've grown up with it. I read a lot of dys-
topian fiction. It's dark, but somehow it normalizes what's
scary. And I think we'll find ways to adapt." He's an unusually

thoughtful kid but also, I believe, fairly representative. He's aware of the world and its present perils, and he's also young, and hopeful, and choosing life.

Our grandchildren are beginning their earthly journeys at a particularly challenging time. If you're reading this book, chances are you and your grandchildren enjoy some degree of privilege: access to health care, food, education. Even so, in their time on earth, they will likely see the consequences of global crises unfolding in scary ways. Yet they will also likely witness—and participate in—new kinds of ingenuity and resilience and hope. It's hard to imagine what coping skills they might need, but it's our job to imagine it.

Part of our work as elders to these little ones is to help equip them for what comes. Small children are capable of surprising depths of understanding and acceptance when we speak to them honestly about sickness, death, or loss. Learning about death and loss may come first with the death of someone they don't know well but may be curious about—a public figure or a friend's grandparent. Or it may come with the death of a pet. It might come with their parents' hard decisions about moving if one of them loses a job, or it might come if their parents separate or divorce. While they're very little, it's not hard for us adults to mask most adult difficulties. But sometimes we have to sit down and talk through hard things with children. They pick up tensions, anxieties, and disruptions in the emotional currents of family life. When those are there, simple honesty is better for them, and all of us, than pretense.

If you find yourself in the position of having to help a small grandchild deal with death, for instance, the Hospice Foundation of America offers good, direct advice about how to do that. Even if a child is "too young" to understand the reality and permanence of death, it's good to avoid euphemisms. Talking about "losing" someone (Why can't we go find them?) or learning that someone "went to be with God" (I need her more than God does!) can be confusing for them. *Died* is a good word to say if that's what's happened, and then you can say as many sentences as it takes to make it clear that the person's love is still real but they won't be coming back. Other straightforward, simple messages put the facts in plain sight and allow children to find whatever questions they need to ask: "He got sick," "She was hurt when another car hit hers," or "He can't see you now, even though he wants to, because he has to be very quiet so his body can get better."

In the few times it's been my hard task to talk to a small child about death, I've come to appreciate the truth of another piece of advice from people who work with grieving children: little ones aren't inclined to stay in grief or horror for long periods. They may continue to be troubled by the trauma, but in the moment, they may want to play. They may even seem indifferent. They don't know where to put the information, so they may need time to find a place to put it. Following their lead, saying only as many sentences as they're ready to hear, answering only the questions they ask, as simply and directly as possible, seems like the best bet.

We recently kept our grandchildren when their mother went to the hospital for a mastectomy. I had a hard time dealing with my own deep sadness as she said goodbye to them and reassured them, holding them against breasts that were about to be removed. After she left, I held those children too. But within five minutes, they wanted to do other things. I realized then, and later, as she went through chemo and lost her hair and used a walker at home, that they had trusted her reassurance. They taught me a lot in that season of their little lives about trust, resilience, honesty, and acceptance. Parts of it were very hard. Parts were not. Their parents involved them in adaptations and in helping with caregiving in ways that empowered them.

Our prayers for the children we love very likely include some version of "May they be protected from all harm." And may it be so. But when it isn't—when trauma and loss occur—we need to prepare ourselves to enter with our whole hearts into the broken moments.

Suggestions for Grandparents

1. The Hospice Foundation of America has a number of resources, including grief groups for children and guidebooks about seeing children through loss, and the Funeral Service Foundation has helpful materials about children and funerals. You can find more information about both online.

2. Stories about ancestors that include their deaths can lay foundations for healthy acceptance of mortality as children grow. An evening with a few pictures of great-grandparents and simple stories about their lives and deaths can open up valuable conversations about connectedness. Such stories can help children gradually recognize that sickness and death happen and that people who love each other see each other through. That we all get a journey here and then get to go home is a valuable theme to revisit.

30

HELPING MAKE THE WORLD A BETTER PLACE

Shirley

Just remember that your real job is that if you are free, you need to free somebody else.

—Toni Morrison, interview
in *O* magazine, November 2003

A baby is a ticket to cross-cultural communication. I learned this when our own children went with us to Haiti and the Ivory Coast on two different study-abroad programs. The younger they were, the more people of all races and social classes reached out to touch them, sang to them, and laughed

145

approvingly when they tried to speak the language. There is something universal about babies and young children.

The same applies to grandparents. Many of us—with gray hair and a slower gait, pushing strollers and unfurling picnic blankets—catch the eyes of another older-than-average caregiver and give a little nod. We are joined in a conspiracy of invisible support. Sometimes we initiate a conversation, discovering what states we are from, what our living arrangements are, and how long we plan to help with childcare.

When I was living as a grandnanny in Brooklyn, New York, strolling a little blond-haired baby down Flatbush, Fulton, and DeKalb Streets and into Fort Greene and Prospect Parks, I looked for ways to connect my rural, white, sectarian roots to this diverse urban environment. I would hum hymns or sixties folk and rock music and pick up litter as we walked, bringing my childhood and adolescence along as I approached a Pakistani street vendor to buy a banana for Owen and cherries for me.

If I strolled Owen into a restaurant, many of the customers were Black, as were many of the shoppers on Fulton Street. I never heard the word *gentrify* on the street, but I could see evidence of the trend everywhere: new high-rises, the enormous Barclay Center taking over the skyline, and boutique shops and restaurants lining the streets. At night, the homeless somehow found places to sleep.

As more white people arrived in Brooklyn, they brought their privilege and affluence with them, making it harder for Black residents and businesses to afford the increase in rents and taxes. The sense of discovery and excitement over hip new restaurants and bars was shared by some people of color, but the majority—the poor and working-class Black communities—were being displaced. On my long walks, I could see pain on many faces.

If racial justice and economic equality are to improve in Owen's generation, we grandparents need to care about these subjects and talk about them with our children and grandchildren. Have we who are white learned anything from the protests, the books, the films, the essays, and the conversations with Black and brown friends?

If we have not, we will all suffer. Our grandchildren will suffer the most. Inaction is not an option. We used to think that not mentioning race—being "color-blind"—was the opposite of being racist. Yet systemic racism is rooted deep in history, ideology, and theology. Alone, we cannot break any of these paradigms even if we want to. We need one another.

One important thing we can do is make friends across the racial boundaries that divide our nation. According to research from the Public Religion Research Institute reported in 2016, 75 percent of white Americans have entirely white social networks—no people of color at all. Zero. We can think more consciously about our own social networks, enlarging from a base of acquaintances and colleagues. True friends share their families. Grandchildren who can see us enjoying our friends will enjoy them too. Seeing different colors of skin will be normal. The example we set—our interest in Black history, our conversations with friends of many races, our participation in protests—will make an impression.

Should we wait until children are old enough to grasp the idea of racism intellectually—age twelve, for example, or when a child goes into middle school—before we talk about race? No! According to author Jennifer Harvey, adults being silent about race during kids' early childhood is like never introducing vegetables to a child's palate and allowing a steady diet of macaroni and cheese. Children need to be helped to develop new and better tastes in many areas of life. Race is one of the most important. Conversations about the beauty of all colors of skin and appreciative exposure to people of other races and cultures should begin before the first birthday and continue in age-appropriate ways thereafter.

Researcher Yair Bar-Haim and his colleagues, in a 2006 study, tell us that as early as three months of age, babies begin to notice and express preference by race. Between the ages of three and five, children begin to apply stereotypes, categorize people by race, and express racial bias.

Our grandchildren will do what we have done: weave their values from the past into their present and future identities. Let's give them stories, toys, and songs that make racial justice and inclusion the norm. Let's take them with us to peaceful protests. Let's let them see true friendships that shake up the hidden, racist boundaries that keep us apart. As Margaret Mead famously said, "Never doubt that a small group of thoughtful, committed citizens can change the world. Indeed, it is the only thing that ever has."

Suggestions for Grandparents

1. *Raising White Kids* by Jennifer Harvey and *Raising Antiracist Kids* by Rebekah Gienapp are helpful books for white grandparents. The podcast *Code Switch* is a great resource for people of all races. There are great lists of antiracist children's books and flashcards online. Some of the ideas in this chapter came from "103 Things White People Can

Do for Racial Justice," an August 2017 post on Medium by Corinne Shutack.

2. Talks by Dr. Lucretia Berry of Brownicity and psychologist Dr. Beverly Daniel Tatum (which you can find online) give examples of how to talk to toddlers about race, why "color blindness" is not possible, and how we end up with color silence instead.

3. It can be deeply satisfying for multiple generations to discuss whether, how, and why to participate in protest movements. Making signs, especially, can provoke good conversation. Children earnestly want to help make the world better. When they recognize that grandparents do too, they will often join in enthusiastically.

4. The Crayola Colors of the World skin tone collection of thirty-two different shades is a great way to get beyond binaries and talk about beauty. If you give a doll to a grandchild, consider a dark-skinned doll and a book with characters of color.

5. Music and sports are places where people of all races and cultures come together. Food, design, art, and dance are some others. Ella Jenkins's *Multicultural Children's Songs* is a great classic. Movies that feature racial breakthroughs in sports, such as the film *42* about Jackie Robinson, are good conversation openers.

TALKING WITH GRANDCHILDREN ABOUT DYING

Shirley

For everything there is a season, and a time for
every matter under heaven:
a time to be born, and a time to die.

—Ecclesiastes 3:1–2

Until the age of four, most children have little comprehension of the idea of death. By the age of seven, they can fathom the three starkest death facts: it is irreversible, the body becomes nonfunctional, and the experience is universal. All of these facts can come as a shock to children when they first learn about them. Often they resist the explanations we struggle to make.

Lydia's encounter with the idea of death began at age three, when she noticed the differences between young and old, fresh and rotten, healthy and sick. She had lots of questions: "Can the doctor always make people get better?" "Why is the celery wilted?" "Where do the tulips and sunflowers go?" "What happens to the compost?" "Will you die, Grandma?" "Will I die?" "I don't want to die!"

She came into the age of awareness of death during a pandemic, but that fact had less impact than the observations she was making of the world in general. The cycle of life and death, which adults take for granted in the natural world, was new, and disturbing, to her.

Fortunately, no one close to Lydia has died yet. Many children move through their teens or even twenties and beyond before they lose a grandparent or other close relative. My son will be forty-five this year, and his grandmother, at age ninety-four, is still going strong. Until someone close to us dies, our knowledge about death stays academic. Yet fear of death can enter long before actual experience does. A shadow falls on a child the first time she hears the words "everything dies."

How can we help our grandchildren develop courage and continued curiosity about a subject so frightening? Can we help them prepare for the likely day that we will die and they will continue on? Though the subject is huge, we can treat it the same way we help them overcome a fear of the dark, of singing or speaking in public, or of going to a new place overnight—by showing them alternate ways of viewing the situation, by taking their hands or hugging or rocking them, and by continuing to ask questions that go behind the first problem to the fear that lies behind it. We must listen deeply, with all of our senses, to what they tell us.

We can also look for opportunities to talk about our own losses and our own hopes for them after we have left this earth. Whether the specter of death is imminent or distant, we can focus on the fact that love never dies. We know we can't be with them in body forever, but we can remain in spirit, cheering for them and helping shed light on their darkest of times.

If we are ill, we can give our grandchildren the great gift of bravery and equanimity. As I write, Owen and Julia's granddad Clayton is moving into the last stage of his life. The children and grandchildren are gathering. He has been more involved with Owen and Julia in the last year than ever before. He and Julia (he calls her J-bird) have read a number of Little House books together and are now reading *Winnie-the-Pooh* while Julia's mother, Chelsea, rolls the video. Someday Julia will look at this video and know that her granddad was overcoming pain in his own body so that he could give her the gift of his precious, fleeting time. All that she needs to know about death will be revealed as she grows older. This video will show her own eight-year-old restlessness and her granddad's steadfastness.

And when she rereads *Winnie-the-Pooh* someday, possibly with her own grandchildren, she will remember that winter's day when her granddad invited her to snuggle beside him for a story.

Suggestions for Grandparents

1. Books are wonderful ways to prepare children for the hard subject of death. The book *The Invisible String* by Patrice Karst is good for children of all ages, including toddlers. The only reference to death is that Uncle Doug in heaven still has an invisible string. *The Next Place I Go* by Warren Hanson has comforted children and adults alike. It is not specifically theological, but it focuses on the idea of a restful place beyond the stresses and sufferings of life on earth.

2. *God Gave Us Heaven* is the story that has comforted many Christian families. Illustrated beautifully, the story shows a papa bear explaining heaven to his cub. *Lifetimes: The Beautiful Way to Explain Death to Children* is a straightforward treatment of death, probably best for children ages eight and older. *The Memory Box* helps children who are grieving the loss of someone very close accept the harshness of separation while providing the hope of lasting memory and connection through eternal love. *Anna's Corn* is a lovely story about preparing a child for a foreseeable death.

3. Letters, like photos and videos, are another way to cheat death. Have you thought of attaching letters to children and grandchildren in your will? Or perhaps you can keep a journal for each grandchild in which to record activities you do together, questions and stories you have been asked or told, and samples of writing or drawing along with your thoughts and comments. These you get to leave behind, and your grandchildren can trace the love you have for them in your thoughts and in your handwriting.

PART IV
GRANDPARENTING
BY HAND

I miss him still today: his long, whiskery eyebrows, his huge hands and hugs, his warmth, his prayers, his stories, but above all his shining example of how to live and how to die.

—Bear Grylls, *Mud, Sweat, and Tears*

32

PROPERTY RIGHTS

Marilyn

There are some things you can't share without ending up liking each other.

—J. K. Rowling

A story still circulates in our extended family about one cousin who, at the age of four, was asked to share his toys. In response, he solemnly announced, "To tell you the truth, I don't share." It seemed a rather dignified position statement. He had considered the matter and concluded that sharing was not going to be his way of dealing with his growing circle of siblings and cousins. He has since, I'm happy to report, revised that position.

Sharing is hard. The roots of what has been called hypercapitalism drive deep into the unconscious mind of even the most generous-minded among us. A sense of property rights starts almost as soon as a sense of self does. "Mine" often appears among the first of a child's spoken words and retains a certain pride of place in the active vocabulary of most toddlers. So teaching a child to share is challenging. It's counterintuitive. Sharing requires a secure enough sense of self to know you can "afford" to let go of something you value and a deep enough trust that what you share will somehow be restored in due time—not an altogether easy lesson for any of us.

When we're taking care of more than one child at a time, as is generally the case when grandchildren come, we open the toy cupboard with a reminder that they can either play together or take turns. If they find it hard to share, they're expected to set up play spaces in different parts of the room and use separate crayons or blocks or cars. That all works to a point, but it's usually not long before one or the other wanders over to see what his brother or sister has, and curiosity quickly turns to covetousness and then into a property dispute.

We continue to model and teach sharing: offer others the cookie plate first; invite your sister to help move around the action figures; put the colored pens where you can both reach them; take turns on the swing. And as I watch them work things out, I'm aware that their efforts to share, and mine, are a lifelong learning. Before he or she is in kindergarten, the average North American child spends about four thousand hours looking at screens, on many of which he or she is assailed with ads carefully aimed at the preschool "target market." "Own your own" is a refrain they're likely to internalize right along with "Say please and thank you."

Families are one of the few places left where the idea of "the commons" survives—things or spaces that can't be individually owned but are held in common for the common good. As more and more public spaces and institutions are privatized, the notion of the common good and awareness of what we hold in common diminishes. Unlike village cultures in many parts of the world, where collaboration and some common property are a matter of survival and where care of children is shared among a circle of familiar adults, a lot of us function in small family units, in homes that are easily closed off, locked, and secured against theft and intrusion. A lot of us have sufficient resources to have at least one of everything a child might need on a visit: one box of art supplies, one box of Legos, one bookshelf with one copy of each book we hope they'll read as they snuggle up with us. They may have to share with one or two siblings, but until they go to preschool, many of them will likely, by cultural default, enjoy fairly unchallenged property rights.

Caring for these little capitalists may be a good opportunity to introduce a gentle challenge to assumptions we want them to question early and often. There are small, simple ways to do this: substitute "ours" for "mine" wherever possible, take them with you when you take garden tools to neighbors or drop off food for a sick friend, let them talk about who we can surprise with the cookies we're baking as we count them out on the baking sheets, and help pack bags of supplies to be distributed to homeless people. One organization in our town collects stuffed Christmas stockings for families living on the margins; stuffing them is a valuable holiday ritual that even the very little ones can be part of. Conversation that moves the focus from "what belongs to me" to "what I belong to" may be one of the best foundational practices to help equip them for life in a culture whose overconsumption will very likely have to change in their lifetimes.

And if we do it well, our grandchildren may discover—and we may be reminded—how much pleasure, liberation from anxiety, and loving relationship comes from opening the grasping hand. We can find much joy in opening our hand and offering what's in it to someone else—someone who may be beautifully surprised.

Suggestions for Grandparents

1. Several books about sharing may be helpful in opening a conversation on the subject: Catherine Rayner's *The Bear Who Shared*, Anna Dewdney's *Llama Llama Time to Share*, and Mike Reiss's *The Boy Who Wouldn't Share* are just three of the many valuable read-alouds on the topic.
2. It can be helpful to make a game of sharing—a kind of scavenger hunt: Find ten things to share in the next ten minutes. Deliver them to another person at the table. Then choose the favorite thing that was delivered to you and say why.
3. In the process of helping kids learn to share, we can reflect for ourselves on the tension between ancient wisdom about sharing—in which hospitality and generosity, gleaning and giving figure prominently—and the culture we inhabit. A few helpful books to fuel such reflections are Luke Timothy Johnson's *Sharing Possessions*, Brian Mclaren's *The Dust Off Their Feet: Lessons from the First Church*, and Heather Menzies's *Reclaiming the Commons for the Common Good*.

33

MAY I HAVE A WORD?

Marilyn

Literature is equipment for living.

—Kenneth Burke

By the time Tommy was four, he had learned to love the library. An early speaker, he delivered full sentences with endearing deliberation and pleasure. He knew then, as I hope my students in English classes know, that a good sentence is a satisfying thing. On the way to the library one day, he asked, "Amma, when we get to the library, may I use the computer?" He knew by then exactly where in the children's section to find the little computers with brightly colored keys and simple word-game programs. "Sure," I responded, "if one is available." He was quiet for a moment, and then I heard him mumbling, "Available. Available. Available." This lasted until we parked. I didn't interrupt him. He was obviously enjoying the word. Savoring it. Trying it out. Perhaps imagining ways to use it.

Tommy's fascination with words may have been unusually acute, but I believe, as Maria Montessori did, that all young children go through a period when their sensitivities are particularly attuned to language. It's amusing and gratifying to hear our words and expressions mirrored by small speakers—though it can be a source of embarrassment when they come out of the mouths of those babes at just the wrong moment or in the wrong context or company. I realized again on that trip to the library how children receive words as gifts from the adult world—how they play with them, try them out, and turn them to new angles and their own peculiar purposes. I realized any sentence I spoke in his presence might contribute to the growing repertoire of words he would make his own and use to navigate the complex world around him. I realized that I and the other adults around him were constantly modeling ways of using words to forge relationship, get what we needed, comfort, amuse, guide, protest, and raise questions. I realized the magnitude of that responsibility.

Conversation was one of the great gifts my own grandmother gave me. She took time to sit down and talk with me, often while peeling potatoes for dinner, but sometimes with nothing in her hands or open lap and nothing on the agenda other than listening to what I might have to say. She asked good questions: "How do you plan to do that?" "Are you going to ask anyone to help you?" "What makes this your favorite chapter?" "What do you think might happen next?" When I responded, she often had another question, or sometimes an observation of her own. She didn't treat me like a peer—far from it. She was an elder, and honoring elders was a clear and well-established value in our household. But she did treat me with respect and brought to our conversations a quality of active interest and curiosity that never trivialized what I had to say as simply "cute."

I have remembered that. Honest interest and engagement with a child's thoughts and observations are important ways of helping her feel loved. When I think of my grandmother's love, I remember first not the cuddling—though I spent plenty of sweet time on her lap—but the conversation. She loved words and taught me to love them by using them, pausing over them, defining them, and inviting me to notice the ones that were especially juicy, angular, or beautiful.

I think of her as children in car seats now regale me with stories about their teachers or about what "mean" kids did on the playground. We talk about what might make someone "mean." They sometimes acknowledge that the person who seems mean may be "frustrated" or "disappointed" or even just sad in ways he or she doesn't know how to express. We talk about how it helps to have words for what you're feeling. When we're reading together, we talk about words we might not use but love to encounter: *punctilious, impecunious, perilous*. We share a certain pleasure in words that reach back to earlier times and other places, words for what knights wore and carried or what women used for weaving and spinning, words for the parts of an explorer's ship or for Native American ceremonies and customs. Some words that come up in stories may seem a bit of a stretch for small ones, but they widen the world for them and give depth and texture to the backdrop against which their own little daily dramas play out.

We do not live by bread alone. The words we give the children we love are as important as snacks and snuggling and visits to the park. One of my dearest hopes as a grandmother is to be in authentic conversation with each of them for all the years we have, intermittent as it may be. It's a good discipline for me to devise questions that surprise them into new avenues of reflection, sentences that make them stop and laugh, and stories that make them want to tell their own. One of the ancient meanings of the word *converse* meant "to walk with." I love that understanding of what we do when, as I did with my grandmother, we just take a little time to "visit"— a word that, itself, is becoming rather quaint but that has a wonderful history of meaning. *Visit*: to come to, to offer comfort or benefit, to inspect or examine, to notice or observe, to see.

One of my daily prayers is that I might really see what's right in front of me, hoping I might at least approach Henry James's ideal: to "be a person upon whom nothing is lost." That ideal sets a high bar, but what a good objective to hold for ourselves and our children and theirs. In a world in which distraction diminishes the quiet we need for reflection and deepened awareness, we can listen for the word that is fitting and helpful—or, as the old *Book of Common Prayer* put it, the word that is "meet and right."

Suggestions for Grandparents

1. Even if kids are distracted, it's possible to clear short spots of time for conversation. It helps to have a particular place—a favorite chair or sofa or a kitchen table—where the invitation that begins, "Come tell me about . . ." may introduce a few good questions and exploratory musing and entertaining anecdotes, even about very ordinary things. It can help to keep a list of questions to try that sidestep those old, often uninspiring, and predictable questions: "How was school?" or "How was your day?" One way to start the list is simply to list the six question words—*who*, *what*, *when*, *where*, *how*, and *why*—and see how many questions you can invent that might be fun to play with. Sometimes instruction can be part of the conversation with very small children: "I'm going to ask a question, and then you can answer, and then I'll answer, and we'll see what we can find out."

2. Introducing a new word can be a little ritual for children one sees regularly—every week a new word, a story about that word (easily retrieved from online etymology dictionaries), or a story about how you encountered that word and why you liked it. It can include a challenge to find a way to use it twice in the course of the afternoon.

3. Reading books about words is a wonderful way to restore the wonder of language. A couple worth knowing about are *Frindle* by Andrew Clements and *In a Word* by Rosalie Baker.

34

WILL YOU BE MY VALENTINE?

Shirley

She's somebody's mother, boys, you know,
For all she's aged and poor and slow,
And I hope some fellow will lend a hand
To help my mother, you understand,
If ever she's poor and old and grey,
And her own dear boy is far away.
     —Mary Dow Brine, "Somebody's Mother"

I always call my mother on Sunday afternoons. She lives in a Pennsylvania retirement community near the farm where I grew up. Soon she will celebrate her ninety-fourth birthday. She enjoys good health and independent living. Like anyone her age, she has suffered many losses, but our conversations almost always focus on how grateful she is for her family—her five children, thirteen grandchildren, and twenty-one great-grandchildren. As we were finishing one recent phone conversation, her ninety-year-old brother, her last remaining sibling, was ringing the doorbell.

One of my roles as a grandmother is to make sure my children and grandchildren honor their great-grandmother, visit her when they can, and include her in stories and celebrations whenever possible. Whenever I tell her about Lydia's love of dancing, Owen's latest photographs, and Julia's books and paintings, she responds with love in her voice—the love that I have always felt from her.

Today she said to me, at age seventy-two, "You are still my little girl."

"Yes," I said. "And now my little girl has a little girl."

Mother and I communicate very simply now. She's hard of hearing, and her short-term memory flickers. Her long-term memory, however, is amazing. When I told her that *The Writer's Almanac* poem of the day was one of her favorites, "Somebody's Mother," she proceeded to recite all thirty-eight lines by heart!

Later in the conversation, Mother reported that she had just stayed overnight in the home of my niece, playing with her five children ages three to twelve. For one night, she left her quiet little apartment behind and basked in the high-energy environment of her granddaughter's large, new house. Her great-granddaughter celebrated her fifth birthday while Mother was visiting. Mother no longer remembers to buy cards or gifts for her huge family, but nobody cares. She wrote out her blessing for her great-granddaughter on a piece of lined notebook paper and placed a five-dollar bill and five one-dollar bills under it. She signed her name. That was more than enough.

I will be seeing Mother in person this week, taking a potted amaryllis halfway to the bloom stage and chocolates in a heart-shaped box. I know her eyes will light up with pleasure. She loves getting presents.

In anticipation of the upcoming holiday, I asked her to tell me, again, a story I remember well from my own childhood—her vivid memory of February 14, 1935: "My third-grade teacher was Miss Gundrum. She was kind, not very tall, and always made the classroom a happy place to learn. The day I remember best in her class was the day we made our own post office out of cardboard and placed it over her desk. In the middle of our 'post office' was a slot. We brought valentine cards for our classmates and put them in the slot. Then postal 'helpers' delivered all the cards to our desks while we sat on our little pink chairs. I felt important and loved."

I can only hope that the stories I've told my children will get a second and third chance to resonate as Mother's have. She is still comfortable with a group of little ones sitting at her feet. Just being in her presence is enough for children to sense many generations of love.

I try to tap into my reservoir of mother love when I anticipate holidays. Sometimes Granddad and I have to send love in the mail instead of holding love in our laps. We will not be seeing any of our grandchildren on February 14. Valentine's Day and Halloween are care-package holidays for us.

As we picked out cards, chose little presents, and wrapped up the packages, we were sharing the residue of long-ago gifts. We hold our place now in a line of ancestors that stretches back to the very beginning of time. It is ours for a very short time. As long as any member of an older generation is still with us, we rejoice.

If we should live long enough to be great-grandparents ourselves, we would do well to imitate the example set before us in the person of my mother. She's more than "somebody's mother," you know. She's mine. And now she's yours too.

Suggestions for Grandparents

1. If you have grandchildren close by, you can turn holidays into opportunities to make things—cakes, cookies, paintings, crafts. Pinterest can give you ideas. The fun can be extended to others also: "Who do we know who is not in our family who might enjoy getting a valentine from us?" Or "Do you know anyone who got left out at school today?" Or "Would you like to cheer up people at the nursing home?" Red and white construction paper and good scissors can make great cards to share.

2. If your grandchildren live too far away for a visit, make a care package to send in the mail. Tailor it to interests and values the child has already developed. Our local fair-trade store had a sale of items from India. We picked out painted stone hearts, bejeweled ink pens, and tape measures to put in a special package with handpicked cards for each child.

3. Like most holidays, this one connects kids to candy. You may or may not want to add to the sweet treat pile, so

you could include alternatives to candy such as fruit snacks. Or if you give candy, try to find ways to make it meaningful. We wrapped up a single larger-than-usual Hershey's Kiss for each grandchild, for example, with a paper family tree that illustrates how our grandchildren are distantly related to Milton Hershey, founder of Hershey's chocolate. We have a common ancestor born in 1719. Maybe Owen and Julia will pick up on Granddad's hobby of genealogy.

4. Seed packets make great Valentine's Day gifts. They can get started on the windowsill and get planted outside later.

5. Valentine's Day is a great opportunity to share the story of how you and your spouse met each other. Children and grandchildren know that they would not exist if some special force would not have brought you together.

SIMPLE GIFTS

Marilyn

'Tis the gift to be simple, 'tis the gift to be free
'Tis the gift to come down where we ought to be,
And when we find ourselves in the place just right,
'Twill be in the valley of love and delight.
                              —Shaker song, 1848

Under considerable pressure from companies targeting the "two-year-old market," small children are learning to want big things: iPads, training bikes, video games, things that squeak and ding and provide instant feedback. They're also learning that holidays come with an infusion of sugar: candy canes, chocolates in bright metallic packaging, prefab gingerbread houses complete with gumdrops, frosted cookies, and flavored popcorn. Advent calendars come with chocolate behind every perforated pop-out door. Amazon encourages parents to post "wish lists" for children as guides for, say, grandparents who wonder what might make the little ones happy.

In a book called *Hundred Dollar Holiday*, Bill McKibben, the widely recognized climate activist who is also a Methodist Sunday school teacher, makes a case for reclaiming Christmas from those whose first concern is sales. McKibben recruited students, local family folk, and church people in an effort to celebrate the holiday with "a seventh or an eighth of the normal American materialism" by spending no more than one hundred dollars for the occasion. That would mean, he candidly pointed out, fewer "Popguns! And bicycles! Roller skates! Drums! Checkerboards! Tricycles! Popcorn! And plums!" Not to mention "PlayStations, Camcorders, Five Irons, and various Obsessions." (The book was published two decades ago; it's possible the proposed spending budget now might be three hundred dollars, and the toys in question proportionately more electronic. Still.) In response to his efforts, local merchandisers and other defenders of more commercial forms of Christmas joy labeled McKibben a grinch and a dour do-gooder.

I admire McKibben for his sustained outspokenness about the linked habits of consumerism and carbon production. With nine grandchildren, I haven't managed to stay within his proposed holiday budget. But like most aging Americans, we are on a budget. I also think the holiday season is a time to revisit messages about humility, simplicity, and caring for the poor and the warnings about getting and spending found in the Gospels and nearly every sacred tradition.

The challenge of shielding small children from aggressive ad campaigns can be daunting, but not impossible. Though we give our modest share of duly wrapped and labeled items chosen from wish lists for Christmas, we've also, with their parents' help, taught them to look forward to experiences, not just "stuff." Tickets to children's theater productions are generally affordable, for example. An at-home game night with a break for inventing toppings for popcorn or a craft evening with supplies for making candles or decorative containers make good gifts. We give the younger grandchildren small things—edibles or rubber balls or large beads for stringing—in little bags hidden not-too-strategically around the house for a treasure hunt. We love decorating the bags and witnessing their delighted discovery.

As they get older, of course, their desires (and devices) become more complicated. But with collective effort, we've managed to hang onto the message that story and song, lingering meals and a few long evenings when busy adults unbusy themselves, and candles at church and walks by the river are all celebrations. We ourselves ask them to put time rather than money into our gifts—to come over for a pancake breakfast and tell us something we don't know about their lives. To help wash the car and then hop in it for an excursion to buy supplies for the meal we're going to make together. To help plan that meal. Sometimes they have other things they'd rather do, but once they come, they're glad. And we're glad. Though it can take a bit of defensive maneuvering to reclaim the time and mental space from more compelling distractions, we learn that doing simple things together can still lift all our hearts.

That the giving and receiving isn't just about or for family seems to me an important part of the message—and one I've loved watching our kids reinforce. Taking cookies to neighbors is one simple gesture of inclusion. Beyond that, I've been gratified to see one daughter involve her boys in choosing and installing decor for a room in a new local refuge for women and children fleeing abusive situations. Another has encouraged two of our grandkids to help us make "angel bags" of supplies for homeless people—pens, paper, protein bars, tissues, toothbrushes, grocery gift cards, and hand sanitizer. Little ones can go along on a special grocery run for the holiday food drive.

Sometimes all this "simple giving" gets challenging. It can be easier to spend money than time and waning energy. Simplicity itself is costly that way. But what better time than the holidays to embody and model what it means to love one another, to receive all guests as Christ, and to pay it forward? What better time to reject the "getting and spending," in the words of William Wordsworth, by which we "lay waste our powers"?

We exercise power in the lives of our little ones. We are mythic figures in their pantheon. Even after they discover our feet of clay, we enjoy a special status among the elders who will help them on their journeys. As we sing our carols, the best gift we can give them may be a wider understanding of joy and of the "world" for which we wish it. The holidays are a good time to teach them that what is not shared is wasted.

Suggestions for Grandparents

1. Small children, and even bigger ones, can enjoy pretty ordinary things if they're undertaken as a special effort to make time together. In addition to those listed in this chapter, some of those ordinary activities easily transformed into fun include making paper napkins into animal shapes for a festive meal; collecting egg cartons, corks, paper-towel spools, and other craft materials for the local family shelter; and scouring closets for contributions to clothing drives. All can become occasions for memorable conversations.

2. One fun alternative to the Christmas wish list is to work together on other kinds of lists and deliver them along with—or as part of—a simple gift:

   7 things I hope for you this coming year
   3 nice things about you that you may not think I've noticed
   5 stories I'd like to hear again
   3 things I'd like you to teach me

   And so on. Lists are always better when written on paper whose margins are colorfully decorated!

36

GOTTA SING

Marilyn

You gotta sing when your spirit says sing . . .

—Raffi

At our mother's funeral, my brother and I, who had written our eulogies independently, both began by recalling the hymn she used to sing us as a lullaby: "Trust and Obey." It was the first of many hymns we heard many times growing up in a lively, loving, pious Christian home.

I have carried many of those hymns with me on my long, winding spiritual path, and they continue to open my eyes and heart. Later I widened the repertoire to include songs that got us through the Vietnam War, songs that fueled my earliest romantic fantasies, songs that were featured in the lively musicals we drove to LA to see on the big screen. Lines from those songs—sometimes whole verses, sometimes just snippets and phrases—come back to me when I need them. They equip me. They meet me in moments when I need not just a word but a melody that carries that word to a place of pain or longing.

As our children were growing up, we sang in the car on long trips. (The one forbidden number being "99 Bottles of Beer on the Wall." Now I forbid it to grandchildren, for whom it is a fresh and unfortunate discovery. Not in my car. It's not the beer—it's the ninety-nine verses.) They learned to sing rounds and to sing parts. One of them still sings when we make dinner together; it's as natural as tying on an apron or slicing bread. (She does a great Judy Garland: "If you gotta sing, sing!")

My voice isn't what it once was, but I sing with the grand-children, too, when the occasion allows. They need to hear us sing. They need to know songs. For many American chil-dren, growing up without church and in schools where music programs have been truncated or cut altogether, song is something of a novelty. Songs are what you can "play" on a device—prefab, commodified, and often overpowered by heavy instrumentation rather than something you sing your-self. It's a deprivation I witness with sorrow and a certain determination to reintroduce song where I can.

The National Association for the Education of Young Chil-dren offers one of many testimonies to the importance of singing to and with young children. Their website includes a list of "Ten Ways Babies Learn When We Sing to Them." Those include bonding, in which your voice becomes a source of security and comfort. Songs also help through transitions:

morning songs or evening songs that provide a ritual for moving between sleep and waking. Through song, children learn rhythm and rhyme—elements of language that attune them to the ways speech itself communicates through rhythm and repeated sounds. And song teaches listening skills: children listen differently as they hum along, learn the words, and move their bodies. Singing ultimately helps make them better listeners. Song is, they also learn, one of the forms love takes.

Singing to grandchildren puts a seal or stamp on the particular relationship we have with them. They have favorites we taught them: "Mama's Takin' Us to the Zoo Tomorrow" and "I'm Being Swallowed by a Boa Constrictor" are particularly appealing to boys of a certain age. And songs that involve body movements ("Head and Shoulders, Feet and Toes") energize them, and us. When someone starts up a favorite, there's often a slight collective mood shift. We all know what to do. That alone is a lovely little bit of community-building.

If someone plays the piano or recorder or has a handy small drum, so much the better. Beating time is an echo of the sound of life. The first thing we hear is a heartbeat. I love the line from a Richard Wilbur poem that is also a prayer for a more loving gaze: "Charge me to see in all bodies the beat of spirit." I wrote a reflection one time on the word *Beat*, a bit of which may bear repeating as we think about song and dance with small children:

Crying babies, I'm told, can be quieted not only by being held close to a human heart, but even (though less cozily, to be sure) by setting a metronome or a ticking clock nearby. One of the earliest forms of play we engage in is to beat on anything in sight; every parent knows the sound of a rattle beating on crib bars or a wooden spoon on a pan. What we're doing, in our wise baby way, is tuning in to the rhythms of life with emphatic declarative trochees that assert our place in the world: "I'm here!" "I want!" "I can!"

A. A. Milne's poems and Dr. Seuss's long verse tales offer their own kind of musicality. Reciting to children is probably rarer than singing to them, but a great gift. They won't soon forget the enlivening beat of conviction in "An elephant's faithful one hundred percent!" or the sound of reassurance in the lilting line, "Wherever I go, there's always Pooh. There's always Pooh and me." When I hear Psalms chanted or sung in any of a wide range of composers' renditions, the original sound of my grandmother reading them becomes a kind of descant in my ear.

Our young ones know our voices even before they know our faces—each one of them sounding its own line in the background chorus against which their life stories will unfold. The gift of our voices, however raspy or off-key we may think they are, will stay with them like birdsong. Heard behind the noise, our songs will vibrate in their cells when we are gone.

Suggestions for Grandparents

1. Not all songs we sing with grandchildren have to be "kid" songs, though it's fun to do those. Hymns, even those with a vocabulary they don't yet understand, are great to grow into. Taking them to church or to some other place where

people are singing together is an important way of helping children imagine and experience intergenerational
community.

2. One timeless and fun album of songs for children is *Peter,
Paul and Mommy*, a 1969 album of songs by the group
many of us grew up loving. Fatherly.com has online a
list of "50 Best Kids' Songs Almost Any Parent Can Sing."
There are other such lists—an inspiration to make your
own playlist.

3. Children can learn simple recitations and be invited to
share them in adult company. To encourage them, and as
a way of playing memorization games together, we might
remember poems or pieces we memorized and recite
with them—or learn one together and perform it for their
parents and siblings. A fun way to make a game of memorization when the children can read a bit is to write out
the lines and read them aloud together, crossing out a few
words each time until you're reciting rather than reading.

37

GRANDPARENT CAMP

Shirley

*If one has only one good memory left in one's heart,
even that may be the means of saving us.*
—Alyosha in Dostoevsky, *The Brothers Karamazov*

"Why is this kite the best kite, Owen?" I asked. He was eight
and staying with us for a week.

"Because it's amazing, that's why!"

I was videotaping his adventure in our backyard, starring the colorful kite he had purchased with points earned
from doing chores. That evening, we sent the video to his
parents, and I saved it on the YouTube channel I reserve for
family and friends.

Listening to it again today, I was pierced by his voice—a voice I have not heard in person for nearly five months. No longer a little child but not yet a teenager, Owen doesn't hesitate to sing out in pure joy when he is happy. He's an earnest, sensitive first child, eager to participate.

His seven-year-old sister Julia shows her enthusiasm in slightly different ways, often visual, comical, and even satirical. Stuart and I were getting a chance to observe their distinctive personalities close-up for a whole week.

We had the sole responsibility for them on several previous visits—the first when their parents took a vacation and we stayed in their home as caretakers, following a schedule they had set up. The second time they stayed at our house for a few days when their parents had intensive work responsibilities.

The third summer was when we chose the name "Grandparent Camp," solidifying the emerging tradition into a much-anticipated seven days of adventure. The name has stuck, and we look forward to years of "camping," conferring with other grandparents in our local area and with the children as we create an agenda.

Their parents drove the long hours to our house, stayed for the weekend, and then took off on their own. After a week of "camp," we drove to a halfway spot and met up. The reunion was touching, as parents and children let out their varied, complex feelings and refocused on each other. The children eagerly "showed and telled" about their week, but the energy was now running toward home and away from us—just as it should.

If Dostoevsky's Alyosha was right—that one "good, sacred memory" preserved from childhood has the power to save us—then we grandparents can rejoice. We can add to the store of memories the way grandparents have always done, by expanding the circle of supportive love and by being different from both children and their parents, exploring with them the very place we live but seeing it anew from their eye level.

Alyosha didn't say so, but I think our memories of helping little children now might be as powerful as the ones we recover from our own childhoods. They move into the future, beyond us. Every Grandparent Camp is a new opportunity to stand like Moses on the brink of the promised land with the children who will go there without us.

What will be remembered from weeks like this one? It's hard to know, and it could very well change over time.

I got a glimpse of one of those memories on Mother's Day this year, however. The children sent cards "All about Grandma," with lists of their favorite things. Both of them said that picking blueberries was their favorite activity to do with me. Owen illustrated our morning in the berry patch down to the individual berries on the bushes.

What made the berry picking memorable? It's hard to know, but one possibility is that it was a new activity for them. We had picked strawberries in a patch before, and they had enjoyed both the berries and the mud. But this was the first time for blueberries. I had ordered a copy of the classic book *Blueberries for Sal* and read it to them, but I don't think that was the reason they liked the trip.

Maybe it was the straw hat that cheery Margaret, the owner of the farm, wore on her head, and the rays of the sun that beat down on us, even early in the morning. Or the cool dew on the grass, the cardinals and mockingbirds singing above us, the freshness of the air.

Maybe the best memories are made of all the senses: the pings the berries made as they rattled around in a metal pail. Or the joy of seeing the little blue mountains rise in the bucket as our handfuls began to accumulate.

Maybe it was the taste of warm berries exploding sweetly in the mouth. Ah, yes. What lingers in the mind and heart for a lifetime can never be prepackaged or determined.

I don't have any photos of that day. Our hands and mouths were occupied! It was good to just stay with the experience of the moment and let the senses record instead of the camera. We grandparents love our smartphone cameras, but our bodies are even smarter. Trusting them, we know our memories go deep.

We know from research that first-time experiences are more memorable than seconds or thirds. And we know that sensory impressions can linger long after conscious recall. We know that time and difficulties can be counted on to call forth pleasant memories as well as make it hard to get away from the ones that haunt us.

We trust that our grandchildren will extract their own memories out of all the experiences we planned and all those that just happened. We stand beside them, watching them run into the future, their kites flying above.

Suggestions for Grandparents

1. Grandparent Camp has become a popular phenomenon. A simple online search will yield scores of articles and books. I did a blog post in 2019 you can find at www .shirleyshowalter.com.

2. This subject is perfect for crowdsourcing. Just ask for suggestions on any social media platform. I asked local friends on Facebook to tell me places to explore and favorite activities in the local area. I discovered places I would not have gone but really enjoyed: a farm with a creamery, a potato chip factory, the blueberry farm, and a place for art classes (the children loved having a structured class four mornings of our week). We visited our local swimming pool for the first time. We also went back to many favorite places like the local arboretum, ice cream shops, and the children's museum.

3. Structure helps, especially structure that children can contribute to or edit. We looked up "chore charts" online, for example, to get ideas for meaningful work children can do. They loved the chance to earn points. It gave them the chance to feel more grown-up and less like a child guest. Owen bought his kite with his chore points.

4. If you enjoy social science research on the subject of memory itself, you have much to choose from. I recommend *The Art of Making Memories* by Meik Wiking.

38

GRANDPARENTS AS TEACHERS

Shirley

There is no Frigate like a Book
To take us Lands away,
Nor any Coursers like a Page
Of prancing Poetry—
This Traverse may the poorest take
Without oppress of Toll—
How frugal is the Chariot
That bears a human Soul.

—Emily Dickinson, "There Is
No Frigate like a Book"

No school that I know of offers degrees in grandparenting. Nor do grandparents get certification as teachers of the young. Yet we are enrolled in the task of teaching just by virtue of showing up. We know that children learn most from the examples we set with our own lives. We know that many things we taught our children, for good or for ill, will continue on to the next generation.

Sometimes, however, we become actual teachers. That can happen informally, such as when we share our love of fishing or skiing or birding or sewing or cooking with a grandchild. Occasionally we may get invited into a grandchild's classroom to read a book or tell a story or sing a song, depending on our interests and skills.

During the coronavirus pandemic, however, some of us were drafted into some combination of virtual babysitting and education. In the spring of 2020, after schools shut down and many parents' workplaces closed, whole families were left to fend for themselves. Children had assignments, but they didn't have online school set up yet. At least our two elementary school grandchildren in New Jersey didn't.

During spring break, the week our whole family had originally planned to be in Florida, our son asked if we grandparents wanted to try "teaching" a class for an hour a day. "Sure," we said.

We scratched our heads thinking about what we had to teach. We made a list: creative writing, genealogy, geography, and nature. We sent our ideas to our son—who, frankly, would have approved astrology, virtual spelunking, or macramé if it gave him an extra hour in the morning.

Julia arrived at FaceTime class with one of her cherished "stuffies," a little lamb. She seemed eager for the lamb to participate. So of course, I started to sing: "Julia had a little lamb, / Little lamb, little lamb. / Julia had a little lamb, / Its fleece was—"

"Super dirty!" blurted out Julia.

OK, I said—write that down and draw a picture. I asked Owen if he wanted to write a story as a sequel to *The Bear on the Stair*, a children's book I had written just for him and Julia years ago.

"Yes!" he exclaimed. Soon Julia was writing and drawing and laughing and singing. Owen disappeared. He decided to take a picture of a bear on the stair. Instead of writing on paper, he started typing his story into his computer.

Our lesson plans sometimes fell by the wayside, but we kept making each other laugh and finding creative ways to sing and read together.

Before we knew it, Anthony's face showed up on my iPhone. "It's time for the next class," he said. "Thanks, Mom and Dad." The whole week flew by. The experience was energizing and exhausting.

What did we learn from this one-week experience?

First, that all plans should be held loosely. Second, that the children will guide you to the things they want to learn if you listen and watch. Third, teaching is both joyously rewarding and hard work! Since we were teachers in our previous lives, we had learned all these lessons before, but we had grown a little rusty. It felt good to get our teaching chops back. It also heightened our awareness of the educational potential in all our interactions with grandchildren. This one week with grandchildren seemed like a gift we would not have had if things hadn't gone awry.

Some authors and educators make ambitious claims for grandparents as teachers. Ken Canfield, for example, says, "I'm realizing that the teaching role may be one of the most important roles grandparents play—maybe the most important." Richard and Linda Eyre describe how they have developed the curriculum they want to teach (things they wished someone would have told them at age ten) and then how they initiated a ritual and a list of secrets to share with each grandchild. In their words, "Making a deliberate effort to teach our grandkids the life principles we think are most important is both a responsibility and an honor."

How can the average grandparent face this high calling to be a teacher without becoming intimidated? One thing to remember is that the grandparent curriculum is life itself. Here's where all of us of "a certain age" can shine! We can focus on a "third thing," educator Parker Palmer's name for subjects that embody thoughts through story, song, and metaphor and are not owned by anyone but available to all. A third thing could be a service project at a homeless shelter, a small construction or renovation project, or a video.

Teaching is soul work. Parker Palmer says that the soul is shy. But when we find something we can gaze at together with the children we most love, we have discovered the secret that opens the doors of perception and turns the key to learning that lasts.

Suggestions for Grandparents

1. The online magazine *Grand*, at the time of this writing, is free. I highly recommend it to grandparents. The article

"Being a Secret Sharing Grandparents," by Richard and Linda Eyre, describes how powerful the idea of sharing a secret is as opposed to giving a lecture. It lays out a way to initiate each grandchild into secrets. If they memorize them and can describe how they work in life, they get a smooth stone to keep reminding them of the secret. The first secret? "Joy is the purpose of life and a choice you can make every day."

2. You don't need a pandemic shutdown to create teaching opportunities. If you share this chapter with them, your children and grandchildren may have their own applications of this idea to suggest. Maybe you will want to try something similar during the next spring or fall break.

3. We found "Covid Time Capsule" worksheets on the internet and gave them to Owen and Julia. They were perfect for capturing the imagination and making a great keepsake for the future. When the whole world goes through an experience like a pandemic, it is important to chart the impact and keep some record of how your personal world changed. These children will be telling stories for the rest of their lives about 2020 and 2021. You can find free examples of time capsules online and may want to adapt them or make your own.

4. Short videos are easy to find online and can provide teaching material and conversation starters on any subject you choose. Your grandchildren are already visually literate. Their observations will astound.

STEPPING IN,
STEPPING BACK

Marilyn

*Raised by grandparents: Barack Obama, Oprah
Winfrey, Jack Nicholson, Carol Burnett, Maya Ange-
lou, Willie Nelson, Bill Clinton.*

Two engaging, thriving young people I know were raised by
grandparents. One was orphaned. Another had parents who
were in and out of prison and drug treatment centers or else
on drugs with no treatment; she needed a stable home and
her grandparents provided that. I've met others along the
way with similar stories: about grandparents stepping into

the gap and taking on a whole new season of childcare—its expenses and heartaches and also its great rewards in bonds of love and trust.

Most of us, I hope, won't be called upon to step in to quite that extent. But in a disrupted economy, in which a living wage can be hard to come by and with gig work on the rise, our social contracts are being rewritten. Rousseau's eighteenth-century book, *The Social Contract*, defined the idea as an implicit agreement between individuals and the state to give up certain freedoms for the sake of the common good. We live by such agreements, in the broader culture and in families. We stay on our side of the highway; we stand in lines; we pay taxes; we step back when our children are married and respect their right to make life choices that diverge from ours. Then again, sometimes we step in, giving up the freedom of the empty nest for the good of the children, in whom we all—grandparents or not—have deep, vested interests. We do it for their sakes and for ours. We do it for love.

According to Pew research and other sources, grandparent involvement not only in childcare but in child-*raising*—the day-to-day tasks of transporting them, teaching them manners, preparing their meals, cleaning their clothes and spills, mending wounds, handling emergencies, supervising homework, calming fears, and getting them to sleep—is growing. Not yet as common in the United States as in some European countries, where nearly half of grandparents live in and provide regular, on-site childcare, American grandparents are increasingly filling in time gaps left by working parents. Some are delighted to be a functioning part of a three-generation family system. In much of the majority world, after all, this is the norm, valued and relied upon by all concerned. Others feel more keenly the sacrifice of the earned freedom, flexibility, and rest that retirement is supposed to bring. Others are still members of the workforce while also enabling adult children to work by time-sharing the little ones. The "social contracts" that divide up this work within families cover a wide spectrum, both in terms of practical arrangements and in terms of which exchanges of time, energy, and sometimes money are made explicit and which remain, sometimes uncomfortably, unacknowledged.

My grandparents lived with us and cared for us daily until our mother returned home from teaching school and, somewhat later, our dad came home from work. They ate meals with us and helped prepare them. Grandpa planted and tended the garden. He gave us rides in the wheelbarrow. What it cost them and our parents to share daily life in the close quarters of a small, one-bathroom house I'll never really know. I do know they carried it off with enough generosity and grace to have made us secure in the knowledge that we were loved and looked after and would be regularly corrected by any of four participating adults. That's a good little circle of basic trust.

As a grandparent now, I doubt I'll be in a position to do what they did. For one thing, our kids are blessed so far with enough job security and flexibility to manage pretty much on their own. Two of them live far enough away that all we can do is visit and appear on-screen for FaceTime sessions. Social distancing during the pandemic entrenched that pattern in new, often frustrating, ways. But still, many of us have decisions to make about when to step in and when to step back—and how big those steps should be.

Several factors make those decisions tricky. Sometimes needs arise gradually, though painfully, as in situations of family tension or impending divorce. Often the needs come on suddenly: a child gets sick or injured, a parent's work situation changes and he or she is away more, or a new baby comes and parental leave has been foreshortened. Often our adult kids don't know what kind of help they need until they face the need head-on and realize they aren't adequately prepared. Because we love them and their children, it's easy to say, "Call anytime" and mean it. But when "anytime" comes, our own readiness and resilience may be complicated by the less obvious but equally important demands we face in our own season of life. I know a number of grandparents who have taken on too much and ended up feeling used and feeling resentful, even though they said yes with great love and goodwill. They recognize the overcommitment is partly their own doing.

Stepping in and stepping back need to be recurrent conversations with our spouses and our kids and their spouses. What do we have a right to expect from each other? What do we owe each other? These are questions that may be more easily answered in traditional societies, where work and family life follow more predictable and homogenous patterns. In North American culture, they're questions to work out in sensitive, open-hearted conversation, identifying needs and wishes as specifically as possible.

Specificity and clarity are great gifts. I need to remind myself that it's a gift to my daughter to tell her I really can't change my plans and take the kids on a Friday night when we need to honor a long-postponed dinner invitation with friends we care about. She knows I would come in any emergency, and she also knows what may be considered an emergency. Short of a real emergency, it doesn't go without saying that we're playing backup. It's good to have a conversation about these matters in times when the needs aren't pressing. It's good, over coffee or on a walk, to consider out loud on what terms you're able and willing to step in.

The adult kids we're still parenting can feel comfortable knowing, if we're clear about our own limits and accessibility, that a loving, considered no may sometimes be a way of protecting the energy we need when it's time to say yes. They know that, when we can, we'll say it with open hearts and open doors and open guest rooms for sleepovers and stories.

Suggestions for Grandparents

1. Try to schedule a leisurely conversation—without grandchildren present—to share the hopes and expectations you all bring into "time-sharing" the kids' lives. The most stubborn snags come up when assumptions are made without sufficient inquiry.

2. It's good to proactively offer a list of things you'd like to do with and for the grandchildren. Consider distinguishing between things you're "eager" to do with them, things you're "quite willing" to do with them, and things you'll do in a pinch but hope not to have to do in an ongoing way unless it's a real necessity.

3. In our family, it's been helpful to ask people to specify, when proposing plans that involve them, where they are on the "Eager to Never" spectrum. I'm eager to do that with you! I'm intrigued and curious. I'm willing. I'm reluctant. I'm skeptical and hope I can stick it out. Or: Never . . . no way . . . you must be kidding.

40

USING TECHNOLOGY WITH GRANDCHILDREN

Shirley

Mr. Watson, come here—I want to see you.
—Alexander Graham Bell's first
words spoken on the telephone

I can't get the image out of my head. At the end of a memorable FaceTime conversation, Lydia's three-year-old face went from relaxed to intense. "I want to *go in* the phone," she said. "I want to go to Grandma's house." Suddenly her little feet filled the frame of the phone as she tried to beam herself past the sleek glass and metal into our arms. It nearly broke my heart.

I did the only thing I could think of. I raised my own feet to the phone and said, "I want to be with you too, Lydia."

There, in one exchange, lies the beauty and pain of the role of technology in both bringing us together and keeping us apart.

Unless your house is very close to your grandchild's, you will probably rely on some form of technology to stay connected. In today's environment, you will have scores of options to consider.

Here are a few types of technology grandparents can use in the 2020s: phone calls, video-phone calls (including group calls), email, blogs, texting, social media (Facebook, Twitter, Instagram, TikTok), Skype, Zoom, games, apps (Marco Polo, WhatsApp, Procreate, Readeo—just a few of thousands). To access these, of course, one needs Wi-Fi and at least one of the following: a smartphone, a tablet, an e-reader, or a computer.

This is not an exhaustive list! To a "late adopter" grandparent, however, it might be exhausting just to see so many examples of hardware and software one does not know how to use—or uses with some degree of discomfort or resistance. In fact, a 2017 Pew Research study of Americans over the age of sixty-five indicated that a minority describe themselves as comfortable using technology. About half said they needed help in setting up new devices. Some seniors lack a broadband connection.

Fear not.

We are nearly the last generation of grandparents who are not "digital natives." Some of us spent our lives in work that did not require us to adapt to technology. Some of us learned one or two new things, like word processing and email, and then did not need to adapt more. Some of us managed to get all the way up the career ladder by having assistants and information technology departments either learn for us or give us personalized instruction. The unspoken motto for many in our generation: the minimum necessary.

Our grandchildren are showing us what happens when curiosity meets technology without fear. Young children trust everything and everyone around them, and shiny new objects like iPhones cannot be held at bay indefinitely. A child pounces at first encounter and begins swiping and clicking away, often finding features grandparents did not know existed.

The makers of these technologies know this and have planted "effects" into the camera app just so grandchildren can turn themselves into mice and giraffes—and then teach Grandma and Grandpa how to do it too.

Our fear is not always a bad thing. It allows us to recognize dangers that lurk under the surface of those shiny objects.

As a child in the 1950s and 1960s, I lived out the tension between fear of and fascination with technology because our Mennonite church had rules. The rulebook stated that the radio posed dangers to faith and was to be used judiciously. Television was not to be owned or viewed at all. This was the era of *The Mickey Mouse Club!* Of *I Love Lucy* and *Gunsmoke* and *The Twilight Zone*. Often called the "golden age" of television, the era vibrated with energy, led by this new technology that whistled and clattered and danced its way right into the center of nearly every American home. Almost 90 percent of American homes had televisions by 1960. Some families sat in their living rooms, ate TV dinners, and watched Walter Cronkite, Chet Huntley, David Brinkley, and Howard K. Smith tell us "the way it is."

Not ours. As a child, I sometimes viewed myself as a starving refugee surrounded by gluttons. The term *FOMO* had not yet been invented, but I knew what it felt like to fear missing out. That experience—of living on the "have not" side of what we now call the digital divide—has influenced my view of both the benefits and risks of technology.

Yes, I had books, and I loved them. I had friends and many adults who loved me. They provided escape and laughter and education. But they didn't give me a surefire entrée into conversations on the playground the way the latest episode of *Leave It to Beaver* or a reenacted Alpo commercial could. Nothing else cemented my friends to one another as much as those animated discussions. I tried to pretend I knew what they were talking about, but inside, I felt deserted and voiceless.

My church later relaxed the rules that isolated me so much from my classmates, and I later came to see value in the fact that I played outside and read more books because we had no television set. I was left with a "both sides" view of wanting my own children to feel both boundaries and freedom when it came to technology.

When we can't be present to our loved ones in body, the benefits of technology are obvious. Something of the spirit can come through devices. The gift of language can be shared in multiple ways, including smiles and tone of voice.

We know, by now, that every technology promises a new dawn of community and creativity, none more grandiose than the claims made in the 1990s for the World Wide Web.

Companies promised not to be evil. Yet within two decades, the very companies that heralded the new Information Age stood accused of violations of privacy, allowing foreign interference in elections, creating hostile work environments for women and people of color, and failing to prevent the abuse of children, just to name a few.

One reason to use appropriate technologies with small children is because we can talk about both the good and the bad, helping them learn to manage within limitations we set—preparing for the day that they will set their own limits, even if their peers do not. A tall order, but one that grandparents can help parents reinforce.

Even when the technology is benignly doing what it was designed to do—connect loving people to each other—it can never allow us all the way "in," even if we put our feet on the phone. To truly come "in" to each other, we need to wrap our soft, old arms around those eager young ones and hang on tight.

Suggestions for Grandparents

1. Start with values, not devices. Work with your adult children to decide which forms of technology help you connect to your grandchildren in any given season. For example, when the grandchild is an infant, you may want to see the baby's new developmental milestones while getting an update on how the parents are doing. Later, when you can talk or write or draw with the little one, you may want to focus on things you treasure, like stories, music, bedtime prayers, or plants and animals. At the same time,

you can ask questions about the budding interests of the child and share the work they share with you.

2. Sherry Turkle's books, especially *Alone Together*, include both cultural critique and analysis of the impact of technology on family life.

3. If you are going to communicate with grandchildren online, you will need a computer, tablet, or smartphone. A simple tripod for your phone or tablet can keep your hands free to gesture or read a book or play with toys or games.

4. Any video-chat software will allow you to talk to and see each other. Zoom got a lot of use during the pandemic because it allows text chat, document sharing, and break-out rooms for small groups. Those features may not matter much in the early years of your grandchildren's lives, but later, you might enjoy exploring this and the many other apps and games available. After the age of eight or nine, your grandchild will probably become your teacher!

41

LEISURELY LEARNING

Marilyn

*Our care of the child should be governed, not by the
desire to make him learn things, but by the endeavor
always to keep burning within him that light which is
called intelligence.*

—Maria Montessori

As we awaited our first child quite a few years ago, we read
voraciously. Among the books spilling off the shelf was one
called *Give Your Child a Superior Mind*. We were eager to
do that—use every opportunity to introduce that baby to the
world, play good music in her room, put up mobiles, show
her shapes, and read aloud to encourage early speech. After
a while, we had to laugh a bit at our own eagerness. She was,

um, a baby. She has, I may say, a fine intellect. But so do her siblings, who weren't subjected to quite the same regimen of early learning efforts.

As the children grew a bit, I came to cherish the wealth of wisdom available in Maria Montessori's writings, including the words quoted in the chapter epigraph. The phrase "make him [or her] learn things" gives a pretty good sense of how pushy it got. Over time, I've come to prefer the idea of "letting" children learn. When thinking about our aspirations for the new babies in our lives, other verbs are worth considering as well: inviting, modeling, showing, opening up, and, as Montessori taught teachers to do, preparing the environment so that children can learn what they're ready to learn.

I'm often struck by how often I hear people express their hopes for and approval of children's learning by language like "fast learner" or "quick on the uptake" or "she gets it right off the bat." Very few of us comment with pride on how slow a child might be. Slow has become a synonym for intellectually inferior. Yet slow learning, like slow eating, may carry a value we've overlooked to our collective detriment.

Slow can mean contemplative. Montessori, who taught deep respect for children's spiritual lives, told many stories about how long a child might gaze or sit quietly or repeat the same task again and again if left undisturbed. I've had occasion to remember those stories as I've taken small grandchildren on walks that don't add up to much in mileage but include a lot of long pauses over dandelion puffs or stray twigs or dog poop. We go slowly. Children are processing more than we can imagine in those first years, but, as Montessori writes in *The Absorbent Mind*, in those years, they don't learn incrementally. They absorb learning like little sponges.

What they learn seeps into them—most of it not by means of instruction but by the deep, preconscious noticing that lays down patterns in their amazing minds.

Slow may be better in those first years. Children will soon enough be subjected to competition, measurement, schedules, and a learning system that has them cramming for tests and pulling all-nighters. Perhaps the best thing we can provide for them while they are little, and when they are with us, is quiet spaciousness—open floor space and open afternoon hours when not much needs to happen. A few toys on the floor—not a pile. Maybe a song—not constant background music. A little conversation, and generous silences.

Sometimes little ones mirror back to me what I most long for: peace and clarity of focus. The pleasure of slow, lingering, savoring. The gift of undisturbed time to notice and notice and, finally, know. When they are satisfied, they stop, satisfied. Witnessing them, I am recalled to something in myself that is too easily buried: that quality of childlikeness without which we cannot "enter the kingdom" because we're too busy heading elsewhere.

Suggestions for Grandparents

1. Experiment with this: When you have your grandchild for an afternoon, deliberately create "spaciousness" rather than stimulation and see how he or she responds. See how long you can leave them to their own devices (pun not intended but recognized!). Intervene as little as possible. See what happens in them and in you.
2. If your grandchild is old enough to walk with you, take a walk that is as slow as possible. You might actually say,

"Let's take our time" or "Let's see what we notice" or "Let's stop whenever we want to." It's so easy to set a goal and urge them along. Goal-lessness, for most of us, requires a little discipline!

3. One thoughtful book about slowing down, written to help kids and those who love them understand ADHD, has a wider application for those of us who are aware of the dangers of overstimulation: *Learning to Slow Down and Pay Attention* by Kathleen Nadeau and Ellen Dixon. Another interesting resource is a box of cards called *Mindful Kids: 50 Mindfulness Activities for Kindness, Focus and Calm.*

42

HELPING RAISE KIDS WHO RAISE QUESTIONS

Marilyn

Indeed, the only truly serious questions are ones that even a child can formulate.

—Milan Kundera,
The Unbearable Lightness of Being

If you've spent much time around small children—and as a grandparent, you likely have—you're familiar with the "Why" period. It seems to be a fairly standard developmental stage in early childhood during which one "Why" question leads to another. Why do I have to put on shoes? Because it's cold outside. Why is it cold? Because winter is coming. Why is winter coming? And so on. Left unchecked, the questions lead on eventually to meteorology or math or metaphysics. If you try to answer them all, you're soon out of your depth and beyond the listening capacity of the little questioners. Most of us learn to answer a few and then deflect or redirect or reframe.

But asking questions is one of the most precious habits you can cultivate in children. Authentic curiosity—not yet funneled and tracked and, alas, sometimes suppressed by formal schooling and testing—is a life force. We can help them form that habit by simple question games, even when they're very small. One of those is a simple set of six colorful, homemade cards bearing the six question words: *Who, What, When, Where, How,* and *Why.* In the few stray minutes before a meal or while waiting for a parent to pick them up, you can hold out the cards, face down, and say, "Let's do questions. You start." No topic is necessary. Anything in the room provides a starting place: Why is milk white? Where did Grandpa go? When do you go to bed? And so on. After allowing one follow-up question, it's the other person's turn. Or you may decide to let one question lead to another, which can produce a memorable conversation.

Another kind of question practice involves simply announcing, in response to something the little one has just said, "I'm going to ask you two questions about that." Announcing it rather than just doing it has an enlivening effect: all of a sudden, they are the subjects of an interview. They're being taken seriously. They sit a little straighter. One person I know and love used to appear, at quite a young age, with little lists of things she wanted to say: I have three things to say about that. I have two questions to ask about what you said. Now as an adult, she's president of a sizable company. Just saying. Now I announce and exchange questions with her children.

Though they're not used as widely as they once were, traditional catechisms, with their question-answer format, teach basic tenets of faith. But catechisms also give children questions to grow into and teach them to recognize questions as trailheads: every question starts a little journey. I had the privilege of helping with a children's catechism at one point, and I found it challenging and exhilarating to tailor large questions for small people. The trick is not simply to "dumb them down." Those small people can come up with very big questions. And they deserve answers that, though simplified, are true and substantive and can be returned to and nuanced as they grow. Why do people die? Do dogs go to heaven? Why doesn't God just make sick people well?

Question games serve similar purposes. They invite invention—quirky, offbeat, surprising, straightforward questions—and offer permission. They help children learn that it's OK to ask. They also give us chances to say, "I don't know, but let's find out." Or sometimes to say, "That's not a question I'm ready to answer right now, but I'll think about it, and we'll talk about it when you're a little bit older." Or sometimes, "I'm *so* glad you asked!"

Suggestions for Grandparents

1. A fun gift for grandchildren is a set of cards with questions on them. When you've been through them all, you can add to the deck or pass them to another family and make new ones. It's important that they be colorful. You could

put some of the question cards on the table for mealtimes with grandchildren. Each person gets to pick a card during the meal and either answer the question or ask it of someone else at the table. This makes for some fun variation in mealtime conversation.

2. An approach to faith development in children that is rooted in Montessori principles, "Godly Play," is a wonderful catechetical method. Frequently used in religious education in church settings, Godly Play can easily be adapted for use with visiting grandchildren, if you're involved in their family's life of faith. It involves unfolding a story by raising questions that invite children to speculate and imagine their way into it, and it's lovely to witness children's responses.

PART V
THEIR FUTURE
AND OURS

Never let fear decide your future.

—anonymous

43

A FEW TRUTHS TO TALK ABOUT IN DUE TIME

Marilyn

Not all adults are fair.
Jesus wasn't white.
Some questions don't have answers.
Your choices may be more limited than ours.
Screens distort.
Money matters in ways it shouldn't.
So does skin color.
Fair comes before generous.
Children don't have an equal vote.
They should have a say.

Adults aren't invulnerable.

What other kids get isn't the gold standard.

"Cost" isn't only about money.

A lot of poisons are appealing.

To learn, you have to let go of something.

We live at the edge of mystery.

You can't always get what you want.

Some people can't get what they need.

You're part of the problem.

You're part of the solution.

Everybody does better when everybody does better.

None of us can do it alone.

Suggestions for Grandparents

1. The aforementioned list is a kind of "cheat sheet" that you can tailor according to the key values and ideas you want to communicate to your grandchildren. If you keep your list in a little notebook or a file and look at it now and then, you might find yourself adding anecdotes to some of the items—how a conversation happened, how even a very young child "got" an important principle. The list can be a kind of elder's hope chest—a collection of things we hope they'll learn—and that we can help them learn—over time. Someday it might become a gift to them, perhaps in calligraphy or your own handwriting on a significant birthday.

2. A range of books that help communicate core values to children can be included among their read-alouds to open conversations. Some of these are the Right Now series by Daniela Owen (*Right Now I Am Fine*; *Right*

Now I Am Brave; *Right Now I Am Kind*), Laurie Wright's *I Will Try (Mindful Mantras)*, and *I Can Do Hard Things* by Gabi Garcia.

3. Consider writing a simple book, illustrating some of your own core messages, for your grandchildren. If you're not artistically inclined, stick figures are, in my experience, remarkably well received! I've written quite a few little books on 4 × 6 cards slid into albums designed for photos. Most of them can be paged through with small, insistent fingers and spilled upon with minimal damage.

44

WHEN ILLNESS COMES

Shirley

Everyone who is born holds dual citizenship,
in the kingdom of the well and in the kingdom of the
sick.

—Susan Sontag, *Illness as Metaphor*

Like many grandparents in their fifties, sixties, and even seventies and eighties, I usually feel fit as a fiddle. I take yoga classes, work on weight machines in the gym, and walk three or four miles a day when I am home. I eat lots of fresh fruits and vegetables, small amounts of meat, and wild-caught fish for a special treat. I think of myself as healthy. My mother leads the way as my role model. She's still living independently at age ninety-four.

But in March of last year, I started out with the worst cold of my life and spent many months unable to enjoy any of my most pleasurable activities—reading, writing, and conversing with friends. My sleep was disturbed, my brain foggy. My health suffered when my daughter got sick and nothing we tried seemed to help.

Our daughter, Kate, suffered even more, from a series of rare and chronic maladies with ever-increasing symptoms. As a result of her illness, our whole family learned about the millions of people who suffer from environmental illnesses, many of whom live like nomads in the desert. We were afraid, as Kate's decline continued for months. We took turns providing support for Kate and taking care of Lydia, who tried to comprehend her mother's situation but was frightened and confused by all the changes. Finally, in December, Kate began to get better. She found a diet and medicines that are healing her body and spirit. Our gratitude to God, to our faithful friends and family, and to her doctors and healers rises with the sun every morning.

Illness changes everything, and it leaves no life untouched. In multigenerational families, we expect that the older generations will be the most vulnerable. Statistically, they are, but babies are sometimes born with illnesses or defects in one or more organs. Parents, too, can face accidents or diseases or mysterious ailments. We can enter the "kingdom of the sick," as Susan Sontag called it, at any point in life.

Grandparents can be invaluable when a child is sick. My friend Gloria and her husband, Jim, have provided a lifeline to their children and their children's children, especially when their two-year-old grandson was diagnosed with leukemia. The cure rates are promising for this disease, but the treatment totally disrupts the family. The child must be taken to a faraway hospital for frequent chemo. When he returns, he must be quarantined to protect his delicate immune system. For two years, mother and child must be separated from father and brother. Where do father and brother go? To grandma's house! That means meals, laundry, and (during the pandemic) tutoring. For Gloria and Jim, there was never a question of whether to offer these gifts. They gladly sacrifice short-term privacy and leisure for the increased chance their precious grandson recovers. They may feel tired sometimes, but their eyes are on the prize, not only of restored health for their grandson but also on modeling to their children the value of teamwork. They are raising *future* grandparents. We all are.

When you have spent a long while in the kingdom of the sick, you are changed. You never feel invincible or immortal, as you might have when you were young. You never assume that a young person can't become sick, that you will always live independently, and that all illnesses have known causes and cures. You discover that misinformation and stigmas still cause unnecessary additional pain and that well-meaning people can say hurtful, crazy things.

If you stay healthy yourself, you can become a wisdom figure in the land of the sick. Like they say on the airlines, place the oxygen mask on your own face before you attempt to help others. It's easy to extend yourself beyond the breaking point of your own health when you care for others. We now know how important it is to place yourself in the circle of care.

Extending yourself as a caregiver may not be possible, however, when your own interior resources have shriveled to a pile of dry leaves. I know this dryness, this numbness of the spirit. I know that time itself heals many dry spells and that the enormous energy it takes to remember to eat, to respond to friends, and to seek information that can help heal is worth it! Now is the time to return to your favorite verses and poems, even if they seem too far away to reach your spirit.

The lessons that come from the kingdom of the sick, when we survive the sojourn there, are all the ones you might expect from near-death experiences. The first is gratitude for the life we have. The second is gratitude for the lives of our family and friends. The third is gratitude for the Creator for all life. All is gratitude.

Suggestions for Grandparents

1. Do you have an illness story, or stories, in your family? Have you preserved it in some way? In a diary, scrapbook, or box of cards and letters? These stories might become helpful for a child or grandchild, or for you, in the future. Cherish them.

2. One of my friends made her grandchildren "Sunshine Boxes" during the coronavirus pandemic. She used chartreuse green shoeboxes tied with bows and stuffed with goodies. Inside the box, she tucked in modeling clay, homemade journals, and treats to eat.

3. Now might be a good time to encourage grandchildren to work on memorizing verses or poetry. Join them. Recite your own favorites to them, in person or via phone or video call. These memorized texts can provide solace in future visits to the kingdom of the sick.

NAVIGATING
SPECIAL NEEDS

Marilyn

All children with special needs have a right to be part of a family, a community and society.
—Angela Dare

Both Shirley and I know grandparents who face the challenge of loving children with special needs. The term covers a wide range of diagnosable medical, mental-health, and behavioral disorders, as well as some conditions not easy to categorize or define. Each condition and each case is different. There's a profound truth to Camus's observation that "everyone is a special case." It is, I suppose, a secular variant of the truth I also believe: that every child is a unique being, a child of God, called forth into this world for purposes we can never fully know.

The needs of kids who are living with type 1 diabetes or cystic fibrosis or severe allergies are quite various, as are the needs of kids who are living with autism or ADHD or Down syndrome. And sometimes a kid who falls well within the range of broad cultural notions of "normal" may have very special needs for a while that require "special handling."

As I consider what we know of our grandchildren—each of them, I am grateful to say, in good health so far and usually good spirits—I am acutely aware of the fluctuations of mood and social pressures that even small ones may experience. But when I look beyond them to the children and grand-children of friends who have faced much bigger and more sustained day-to-day challenges that are widely (and legally) recognized as special needs, I am humbled by how they and their families rise to those occasions—and keep rising.

The children I know who need particular care vary. One has slow-growing brain tumors that have affected speech, mobility, and mental functioning. One has cystic fibrosis. One has received multiple behavioral diagnoses and suffered—I used the word advisedly—from violent behavior. Two have parents who are addicts, one an incarcerated parent. One is in a long recovery from very early trauma. I've witnessed some of their challenging journeys at close range and others secondhand, through conversations with their parents and grandparents.

Shirley's granddaughter has mild cerebral palsy, enough to connect the family to others with more profound needs.

Another child in her circle of care has muscular dystrophy. Even when the case is mild or the relationship distant, a grandparent learns much from others whose lives have been turned upside down by a diagnosis yet who manage to stay right side up.

Here is some of the guidance I've gleaned about the demands and surprising rewards of grandparenting children with special needs.

First, you cry. When what are likely to be lifelong problems with breathing or walking or other basic bodily functions show up at birth, there has to be room for your own grief even as you hold and console the parents. The dream of a perfectly formed, perfectly healthy child has to give way sooner or later, but for most, it's gradual. Grieving, even as you're welcoming a little one into the world, is complicated by practical, medical, and financial decisions the parents have to make. Grief is also made more complex by others' reactions, which are likely not uniformly helpful.

Honor the parents' decisions. Parents of children with special needs tend to receive more unsolicited advice and more judgment than most. One of the best ways to be supportive is to accept the logic of your adult children's decisions about care, privacy, and professional involvement. Unless clear harm is being done, grandparents can work with the grain of those decisions. If the parents seem overprotective, our role is still to protect. If they refuse to consider treatment alternatives we think are viable and might be helpful, we need to imagine their exhaustion and need for expert help and reassurance.

Equip yourself. Helping care for a child with special needs requires some education about their condition, about their parents' options, sometimes about the effects of drugs or food allergies, about how to use an EpiPen or a hypodermic or a breathing device, or about how to do postsurgical routines. Grandparents won't usually be the ones on the front line; they won't generally be the ones in the doctor's office getting firsthand instructions. So it's that much more important to ask questions, search the internet, read, and seek out others in similar situations and hear their stories.

Explore, expand, and reclaim the undersung virtue of patience. The needs of children with special needs can be overwhelming. Physical care may be strenuous. Their emotional volatility can be exhausting. If we're going to accept the privilege and challenge of being occasional caregivers, even for a few hours each week, we need to develop explicit strategies, ideally in conversation with the child's parents, for making those few hours peaceful, prayerful, imaginative, and perhaps even invigorating. As someone who hasn't "been there," I cannot claim, without sounding glib, that sometimes a health or mental-health challenge in a child becomes an unexpected blessing. But I have heard this from parents and grandparents who have found themselves "surprised by joy" in the midst of a long learning curve of adaptation.

Watch and pray. Watch—meaning familiarize yourself with particular patterns of need—the child and his or her parents. Watch for the appropriate moment to step in with real help rather than hovering. Watch for indications of unspoken needs that might need to be inferred. And pray, in whatever way you can and do, without ceasing. Let thoughts about the ones you love become a string of moments when you call in the light to surround and sustain them—and you.

Special needs are a special assignment for both the immediate family and grandparents who find themselves, in a later season of life, called back into new kinds of "active duty." Even more than for children whose needs are lesser and more predictable, grandparents of a child with special needs learn when to try to meet those needs and when to let the child enter into her or his own struggle, developing the courage and resilience that will be needed every step of the way.

Suggestions for Grandparents

1. A number of bloggers have addressed the particular needs of grandparents of children with special needs. One that is rich with insight and guidance can be found at www .differentdream.com by searching "special needs grand-parenting series."
2. If you are a grandparent likely to be frequently—or even solely—responsible for a child with special needs, it's helpful to look at the AARP guide for grandparents of children with special needs, which covers basic legal, medical, and practical issues you might not anticipate: https://www.aarp.org/relationships/friends-family/info -08-2011/grandfamilies-guide-getting-started.html.
3. Support groups exist in most urban areas and online for family members actively involved in helping care for children with diagnosable or legally recognized conditions requiring special adaptations. These can generally be found easily with an online search. Community Tool Box provides a handy guide for starting your own support group, if you're so inclined: https://ctb.ku.edu/en/ table-of-contents/implement/enhancing-support/peer -support-groups/main.

46

VULNERABILITIES

Marilyn

We're all in it together.

As we wrote this book, governments and health departments all over the world were scrambling to cope with the coronavirus pandemic. One by one, states and counties were enforcing "shelter in place" orders that confined everyone not working in "essential" jobs to their homes. No gathering. No visiting with anyone outside of the household. If we went outside, we kept a space of six feet between ourselves and others. Unless they lived with us, there was no hugging grandchildren.

I hope that by the time you're reading this, the pandemic will be a thing of the past. But public health crises will not.

As ecosystems are destroyed, new zoonotic diseases emerge. Living with that reality is sobering. Many of us have not had to reckon with the personal impact of those viral events until recently.

I did some of that reckoning as our weekly dates with grandchildren during the pandemic came and went. We met them on FaceTime. I'm grateful for the convenience of virtual meetings, but they're certainly no substitute for nudging and hugging and lighting a candle and sharing a meal at a real table in real time. It's tempting to think, *We're family. We're used to one another's germs. Surely we could get together.* But hard facts had been well reinforced for us: everyone is a vector in a viral epidemic; everyone brings all their exposures with them into each new environment; people over sixty-five are more vulnerable to severe infection than younger people; children, despite efforts to teach them extra hygiene, tend to be careless about sanitation. Strangely, and sadly, we were being protected from one another.

Social distancing makes practical sense, of course; the best science we have suggests that it is an effective approach to curbing the spread of a virulent disease. But it carries a psychological cost. All of us who were separated from the little people whose hugs are so mutually nourishing needed not only to find ways to stay in touch but also, perhaps more subtly, to find ways to speak about the distance between us. We needed to learn ways to describe what was happening that reassured them, and perhaps ourselves, that this would pass, that intimacy is and will be good and safe, that the day would come when we can share a long hug and lap time. That love, in the meantime, was just as real and strong.

It was a tender teaching moment. We have one grandchild who is inclined to become overanxious, sometimes about hygiene. He needs help balancing commonsense precaution against a perpetual fear of germs. I wondered some days how much fear of contact would linger after the crisis is past. We have another who was bewildered and angry by the isolation, which is surely more frustrating for those too young to grasp the bigger picture. Because elders (or—a term I'm not really at peace with yet—*the elderly*) were more at risk, kids were being told to take special care to keep their distance from grandparents. I wonder how much that habit of distancing from us, and from other older people, will linger.

Words mattered as we adapted to the notion that, at least for a time, we might be a danger to one another. We all wanted to provide—and to be—a "safe space" for the children we love. But when it was not altogether safe for us to be in the same space, we needed to find a larger way of speaking about and creating a sense of safety. Conversations about illness itself, curiosity about the science we were all needing to learn, and even here and there a little laughter over the awkwardness of adaptation helped.

Even in times of ordinary illness, simple messages can help small children feel a little more comfortable and a little less afraid. Grandparents who may need to take extra precautions for their own, and sometimes the children's, sake can offer words of assurance and hope:

"Right now, we're not going to hug, but we can sing and play new kinds of games until we can hug again."

"We're all opening up the space around our bodies a little wider so we can help our bodies stay healthy."

"You know how bears hibernate? They go away from everyone for a season and go to sleep. This season is a little like that. We're all staying in our houses for a while. After that, we'll come out and celebrate to be together again."

In an era of a pandemic, we learn the ancient wisdom of feasting and fasting in various ways. We learn that there are times to gather and times to refrain from gathering, for the sake of the other. A teaching moment, indeed.

Suggestions for Grandparents

1. When public health crises occur, as they doubtless will, and health and safety require new behaviors, it's a good time to help children with discernment. This might include messages such as the following: Being careful doesn't mean you have to be scared. Washing a lot more frequently right now doesn't mean your body can't handle most germs most of the time. Staying away from people to protect them can be a way of loving them.

2. Several board books offer useful first lessons about germs. *Germs Are Not for Sharing* by Elizabeth Verdick and Marieka Heinlen, *Do Not Lick This Book* by Idan Ben-Barak and Julian Frost, and *What Are Germs?* by Katie Daynes are helpful and well-illustrated places to begin their biological education.

47

LETTERS FOR LATER

Marilyn

To write is human, to receive a letter: Divine!
—Susan Lendroth

At one point in my schooling, when I was studying the lives of early American colonists, I learned that many Puritan women wrote letters to their unborn children. They were well aware of how many women died in childbirth. The letters were intended to leave a legacy of love and instruction for the children they might never see. Doubtless, some of these were held in trust by grieving fathers and delivered when children were old enough to receive these sad gifts of motherly love.

Fortunately, we and our childbearing children live in a time when much more can be done to prevent mortality in childbirth. But the idea of leaving a legacy of words for children has remained with me since reading those letters. It became more meaningful to me many years ago, when I married a man with children whose mother had died. She left each of them a letter she knew would be among her final messages to them. I have often thought of the value of making conscious legacies not only of money or goods but of words—a legacy that might help sustain those who will very likely survive us.

Our grandchildren will have guides, as we have, who show up in various corners of their lives and help them: teachers, older friends, pastors, oddball relatives, and surprising strangers. But it seems right for us to take our place among them. I want to leave them not only their particular memories of times spent with us, or photos, or even video and voice recordings, but letters to be unfolded and read in some quiet moment.

A letter a grandparent writes to an infant or toddler is likely to sit in a box for a long time. But if it's left unsealed, it can also be a gift to that child's parents—I'm aware of the pleasure our kids take in notes I write to their kids, who are older now. Occasionally I write letters to my grandchildren when I want to address not only their present selves but the people they may become. Without imposing my own specific predictions of their career paths or personality development, I like finding ways to say, "I can see how you're already resilient and ready to dry your tears and come back and play. I imagine you one day as a person who is quick to forgive and capable of finding ways of restoring and repairing when something is broken between you and another person. I hope that for you." Or in another case, "I see already that it's hard for you not to get very angry when things go wrong. I know anger is a kind of suffering. I also know how loving and open-hearted you are when that cloud of anger passes. One of my hopes for you is that when things make you angry, you'll find ways to stop, imagine the other person's story, give yourself some time, and come back to your center where that big heart is."

By observing their behavior even when they're very small, grandparents can find patterns to foster and problems to help equip children for and encourage them through. Your words may not add much to what their parents and other elders are already telling them. But coming from a different distance—and with a slightly different kind of love, historical perspective, and perhaps capacity for humor when others are enmeshed and anxious—your words might just provide something they need at just the time they need it.

I know people who write their children or grandchildren letters each year. When they're infants, those letters are intended for later. Some of them are dated: to be opened on your tenth birthday, on the day you start high school, when you're able to read it for yourself. I wish I had written those letters regularly. (And even as I say that, I realize there's still time!) If I don't, they'll still know I love them. But if I do, those pages, perhaps a little yellowed, might just be unfolded in a moment when, by grace I can't foresee or control, some-thing I say might be just what they need to hear.

My letter might make them laugh. It might make them take a larger view of their own lives. It might release them from anxiety or guilt. Or it might just say, again, what bears say-ing again. You have been held and witnessed and loved by more people and in more ways than you know. You still are.

Suggestions for Grandparents

1. Write the letter! Write it on the day of a child's birth, or on a first birthday, or on a random day when you're thinking about them. It's good to keep it to a page so that the central message doesn't get lost and so that reading it won't look like a chore. Since our handwriting is a unique expression of who we are, it's good to write—or print—by hand, if possible.

2. Writing letters or cards, with one short message and with some regularity, can be a satisfying practice even when children are too small to read them. Their moms or dads can keep them for when they're ready, at which point they'll provide a little record of how they've been noticed and witnessed and laughed over and loved.

3. If you draw, developing a simple cartoon character who reappears in such letters can be an added delight—both for you as you write them and for the child who eventually sees that character as someone who came into being precisely for him or her.

48

MAKE SOMETHING THEY CAN USE EVERY DAY

Shirley

That's the thing with handmade items. They still have the person's mark on them, and when you hold them, you feel less alone.
—Aimee Bender, *The Color Master: Stories*

"You won't find these on the internet!" my friend Joan says, as she plops a three-ring binder into my lap. Then she laughs. The book is one copy of a gift ready to go to her sister and to all her grandchildren. It's chock full of recipes, stories, and pictures of four generations of smiling family members, often with a kitchen or garden as a backdrop. Joan made the books the old-fashioned way: with construction paper, handwritten notes, and photos, each page slipped into a plastic sleeve.

She spent more than a year collecting the recipes and photos, designing the layout, pasting in little illustrations, writing down memories and stories, and making multiple copies of the book. The index to recipes begins with home-made applesauce and tomato sauce, made from fresh produce and canned. Many people never developed or have lost this skill, but Joan cans every summer, using the bounty from her garden. She also hauls apples and peaches in baskets from a local orchard.

Her grandchildren line up to be part of the operation at the sink, table, and stove, learning how to use a knife safely and how to fill jars with just the right amount of fruit. And they use the time together to talk just like Joan did with her mother when she was a girl. In addition to skills in the kitchen, the children are learning things about relationships and resilience.

Joan's mother died recently, at the age of ninety-three. She is the one who taught these skills to Joan and her sister, Betty Jo. Canning and gardening were necessities because the young mother was a widow with two girls under seven years. Keeping the girls with her while she tended their small farm meant backbreaking labor from sunup to sundown. It could have ground the laughter and the joy right out of life. But with the help of her deceased husband's family and their church community, the young widow was able to keep the family together, relying on stories and songs and the strength of faith to carry on. She used every scrap of food and fabric to keep creative new projects in front of her girls, who were learning that they could not only survive but thrive even in difficult times.

Joan brings all this history to her current life as an energetic, enthusiastic grandma. The scrapbooks she has made are already treasured objects, destined to become even more precious as time passes and children begin to comprehend the layers of fierce love woven into every page.

Suggestions for Grandparents

1. As a new grandparent, you can take advantage of the "beginner's mind" that transforms ignorance of this new role into a set of questions to ask more experienced grandparents. Go to the real experts in your life—the friends whose families you most admire. People love the chance to talk about this subject! Here are a few sample questions: How can I give gifts that will last rather than ones that will break? What values are you trying to transmit? How can you use actions in addition to words when you share values with grandchildren?

2. I found this story by using a simple technique called "the interview." I was so impressed by the gift notebooks my friend Joan made for her grandchildren that I asked if she would answer some questions. This chapter comes from weaving her answers into a narrative. You, too, have access to grandparent wisdom through your friends.

3. Maybe you aren't a gardener, canner, or sewer. (At this point in my life, neither am I!) But I want to give my grandchildren some homemade items, nonetheless. Maybe that is just letters and notes (see chapter 47). Get some good stationery and a fine pen. Give your grandchildren

the gift of your handwriting. No one else on earth writes exactly like you do. No one else ever will.

4. Think of things other than cooking that your grandchild might see every day. Perhaps you want to make a note-card with a favorite quotation or your own words for the child to place on the bathroom mirror. Perhaps you want to make a little card to put into a pot on the dining room table with a blessing or prayer for the whole family in it. Perhaps, like coauthor Marilyn, you want to make the pot itself!

49

BECOMING A GOOD ANCESTOR

Shirley

Let us be the ancestors our descendants will thank.
—Winona LaDuke, Twitter, December 6, 2015

My friend Casonya became a grandmother three years ago. By her own account, she was not ready to become an ancestor! An active professional woman enjoying her career as a biology professor, she was not expecting the news her son and daughter-in-law shared with her. "I had no idea what was going to happen," she tells me. But on the day of birth, when she first held her granddaughter, Rowen, in her arms, a transformation took place in Casonya's heart. When she describes that moment, even now, her dark eyes, always curious and alert, shine with intense joy: "I was in love. And in a whole new way."

Casonya has followed each milestone in Rowen's life. One of the activities they enjoy doing together, now that Rowen is nearly three years old, is listening to music, singing, and dancing. A scientist by vocation, Casonya is also a talented musician by avocation. As the granddaughter of a Baptist preacher and the niece of the music director, she grew up with gospel music and spirituals, which she still sings "loud and long." She now has a repertoire and a wide range of musical tastes to share. She delights in Rowen's prowess in working out the rhythm of a piece of music, taking it into her body, and then moving with it as she sings.

Becoming a grandmother has led Casonya to reflect upon what she wants to pass along from her own ancestry. "Family history can be very complicated. My grandmother, for example, didn't talk much about her childhood. I have had to piece together the little I know," she says.

Casonya has learned that her grandmother, Annie, became an orphan at the age of thirteen, after first losing her mother to illness and then her father to an accident. The father's death left seven children alone in the house. Very few families could have survived. But this one did!

Casonya's grandmother was the oldest of the children. She and her eleven-year-old sister took charge. "This was a necessity," says Casonya. "Wake up and do what needs to be done!" The children stayed together by fulfilling the first duty of sharecroppers: farming the land. They also learned to cook, do laundry, and sew. The hard work that allowed the children to stay together had a lasting impact.

In the case of Casonya's grandmother, the determination that drove her to lead her siblings also made her reluctant to talk about her experience. Instead, she developed a quiet strength, relying on her faith in God. Says Casonya, "She lived her faith and didn't feel the need to talk about it."

Casonya has constructed her own faith along the same lines. She hopes Rowen will see the spiritual base of her relationship to the natural world: "I talk to God a lot, and I have favorite verses from the Bible, especially Psalm 34:8, which I paraphrase and think of often: Taste and see that God is good. See it and hear it and smell it and feel it!"

She also aspires to create a "let's talk about it" relationship with Rowen—the kind of conversations that she remembers having with her Grandma Annie: "She was a great listener. So centered and calm. But she also instilled confidence by taking everything you said seriously. She gave me responses without judgment."

Because of those conversations, Casonya says, "For years I believed that I was Grandma's favorite grandchild. Then I discovered that all my cousins thought the same thing!"

Casonya is a young grandma, still working out what it means to be an ancestor. But no matter how many grandchildren she eventually has, they, too, will believe she loves them the most. For that, they can thank their great-great-grandma Annie.

Suggestions for Grandparents

1. The connection between the idea of being a good ancestor and the African American community is a strong one. Layla Saad's book *Me and White Supremacy: Combat Racism, Change the World, and Become a Good Ancestor* has placed the idea of becoming a good ancestor squarely in the middle of the conversation about becoming antiracist. Her podcast is called *Good Ancestor*, and her Instagram uses the same theme. "The primary force that drives my work is a passionate desire to become a good ancestor," Saad writes. How does this idea of becoming a good ancestor inform your calling as a grandparent?

2. What can you do in your community to further the mission? Start a Good Ancestor book club? Supper club? The more diverse the group, the greater the wisdom shared, and the more likely it will be that you will be handing a slightly better world to your own grandchildren.

3. Grandparents united can have a national and international voice. I carried a sign at the Women's March in DC in 2017 that said, simply, "Grandma Power." Sure enough, I met another woman carrying a sign, featuring an image of a mother bear and her cub, that read "Grandmother Power." Even in a society that prefers youth over age, the combined voices of the elders have moral force. Let's use it both individually and collectively.

50

LOOKING AHEAD

Marilyn

It is into us that the lives of grandparents have gone. It is in us that their history becomes a future.
—Charles and Ann Morse

We have written these chapters with relatively new grandparents in mind. But as the oldest of our grandchildren has just come of age, I know we could write an entire book for grandparents about the complicated terrain of the tween and teenage and young adult years.

Our oldest grandchild can vote now. He has to register for military service, which I hope and pray he won't have to enter, given the dubious objectives and destructiveness of the wars we wage now. As I write this, the youngest of our grandchildren is still swimming comfortably in her mama's womb, getting ready to emerge into a complicated world on a wave of love and support we hope will carry her on her journey.

I can't hope in a short reflection to be comprehensive, but I will share here just a few important things I've learned from the rich, joyful, heart-filling, heart-aching hours I've spent with our children's children.

It's not like when we were young. I actually heard this sentence first from my daughter when she stopped me as I began to make an analogy between her current social dilemma and my own high school bewilderments. When she was in high school, teenagers were pressured to become sexually aware, if not active, at a much younger age than when I was an adolescent, and that's true now as well. The degree to which their social life is mediated and made public on social media is, for some of us, almost unimaginable and even horrifying. The amount of standardized testing has changed the terms of success in school. The marketing pressures have intensified conspicuous consumption as a means of self-identification; the thresholds of tolerance for violence on-screen and in song lyrics have risen steadily. Religious self-identification has diminished. Clinical depression has increased among teens and preteens. Trust in public authority has atrophied. Economic disparities have left increasing numbers of families living near or below the poverty line. Climate change looms as a defining apocalyptic problem for their generation.

Our grandchildren will be required to be smarter in some ways than we were. As curricula adapt to the urgencies of their generation, they'll be deprived of some dimensions of education we took for granted. They'll be more techno-savvy, quicker to adapt to change, and more aware of a wider world, although that awareness may at times lack a historical and philosophical depth.

Staying connected takes creative effort. Most of us won't have the luxury of regular three-generational gatherings around, say, Sunday dinner. Some of us may have regular care of grandchildren but may find those hours filled with supervising homework, transporting them to extracurricular activities or playdates, or negotiating screen time. If we're inventive and inviting about it, we may be able to carve out time for reading aloud. Most children enjoy cooking or baking together, especially when the outcomes are delectable. Puzzles, board games, gardening, observation walks—so many activities we've suggested in other parts of this book—are wonderful ways to connect, but they don't happen automatically.

Making sure times with our grandchildren happen with open hearts and goodwill on both sides is a matter of close, ongoing noticing: What does each of them need? What pressures, uncertainties, frustrations, hopes, and curiosities seem to be at work in their lives at the moment? What might they be willing to talk more about if we asked without judgment and really listened? For each child, the answers to those questions will be different at any given moment.

We may have to ask for what we want. It takes a certain humility and courage to actually say to a growing child who seems to be increasingly disinclined to spend time off-screen with grandparents, "Relationship with me is not optional. We have one. It can be either a pleasure for both of us or a drag. I'd like to talk with you about how we can enjoy each other." Or more simply, "I want a real conversation with you. Tell me what times might work for a walk or a half hour over snacks." Or "I give you time and attention and help because I love you. I expect some of your time and honest attention in return." The social contract between grandparents and grandchildren isn't inscribed in most family lore, but sometimes it needs to be redrafted—perhaps repeatedly. This need not be onerous; it can be an occasion for engaging, honest, lively reflection. Hot cocoa helps.

The drip system works. I borrow the metaphor from John Gray, who recommended it to men as a way to help make womenfolk happy: keep the love coming in small ways every day. One big spray of roses on an anniversary isn't going to suffice. "I love you" every day with full eye contact and a real hug matters much more. In the same way, small gestures that keep the door open for grandkids matter more than big birthday presents. Sending on a bit of internet humor you come across, texting a good-luck message on a day you know they're having a test, sharing an odd bit of trivia related to their current interests, offering a fact from your own history they may not have known: such small acts now and then can keep the communication channels open. These things carry a basic message that they are noticed, loved, respected, and enjoyed.

Grandparenting involves lifelong learning. I mean that grandparenting requires all types of learning—not just learning about babies or CPR or healthy nutrition but learning about the world. You need to read enough to salt your own conversation with interesting facts, anecdotes, and recommendations. You need to get news from reliable sources, including something about the science behind alternative energy development or vaccine development or basic economic forces affecting young people preparing to enter the competition for work (even summer jobs). You can learn how to watch the movies marketed to kids with both empathetic and critical interest and raise questions about them that will invite thoughtful responses.

The more homework we do and the more we engage with the world—its problems, its mysteries, and what lies beyond this dimension—the more we'll become more alive human beings. We'll also become more capable of enjoying our own company so as not to need to be needed.

Because we won't always be needed. Those little birds, like their parents, are flexing and squirming, getting ready to be shoved out of the nest—just as their parents did. Our connections with them, even if they run strong and deep, will at times likely be intermittent.

The great "love chapter" in 1 Corinthians 13 lists many attributes of authentic love, but one more could be added to that list. Besides being patient, kind, humble, and generous, love is flexible. As we encircle these grandchildren with our love, that circle needs to grow and shift. Like a healthy river, its banks need to keep reshaping themselves as the flow changes.

The way of the wise person, Lao-tzu teaches, is the "way of water." As we move through our lives and theirs, we may be able to help them best when we attune ourselves to the deep currents of our own desires and faith. As we watch and pray and notice and adapt, we may continue to find new meaning in the wisdom Wendell Berry distilled into a single sentence: "Love changes, and in change is true."

Suggestions for Grandparents

1. As they reach reading age, children might enjoy a "book club," in which they can read a book in common with grandparents and talk about it over the aforementioned cocoa once a week or once a month. There's a lot of fine literature for children and young adults out there, although it requires some sifting to find it.

2. If your grandchildren are among the many who need at least a once-a-season excavation of their rooms—and if their parents are willing—a cleanup date can be fun. Helping them clean their rooms can involve small but meaningful conversations about what's to be kept, donated, or disposed of and why. These chats can become quite personal and interesting as long as they don't involve too many efforts to persuade them to part with apparently pointless plastic doodads.

3. Your older grandchildren may not want help with homework, but it's good to find out occasionally what particular topics are coming up in school. You can then ask germane questions and drop in interesting bits of information that help them remember homework isn't just a chore but preparation for a wider engagement with an interesting environment.

OUR ROLES IN THEIR RITES OF PASSAGE

Shirley

The children must be taught how to think, not what to think.

—Margaret Mead, *Coming of Age in Samoa: A Psychological Study of Primitive Youth for Western Civilisation*

Perhaps one of the greatest gifts a grandparent can give a child is the gift of time made sacred by other gifts—presence, attention, marking, and honoring. This gift can begin before birth, as in the case of the mother blessing ceremony described in chapter 4. It can continue through any other events set aside as special—baptisms, dedications, bar or bat mitzvahs, confirmations, graduations, quinceañeras, and any others decreed by culture, religion, or family tradition.

Rituals or rites occur more frequently in some cultures than in others. When I was a child on the farm, most time was "ordinary" time. Every day, the cows were milked, the seeds were in the ground as soon as the frost was gone, and I could count on seeing Grandpa Hess's old white Cadillac pull into our driveway just before noon every Saturday. To everything, there was a season, and life on the farm responded directly to all four of them.

Years later, as parents living far from our farm homes and families, Stuart and I wanted to create some substitutes for the "thick culture" that surrounded us in youth. One resource was our church, where Sunday school, Bible school, mentors for young people, and youth programs marked passages from infancy to young adulthood. Joel, one of the fathers in our small group (four families from the congregation who met for a meal several times a month), suggested that we create our own coming-of-age ritual for adolescents in our midst. During a meeting close to the time of a young person's thirteenth birthday, we looked through scrapbooks, slides, and videos that documented each previous stage of childhood. We told stories and laughed a lot, noting special patterns in the new teenager's personality. Then came the ritual gift, one that all six of the children in the group received: a wooden box designed and handmade by an Amish craftsman. The box was intended to hold pocket items. Each adult contributed an item small enough to go in the box and a letter that went into a hidden compartment. A hidden compartment symbolizes both the collective and unique elements each child takes into the adult world. It suggests to the child that the inner life is central to the outer life. It adds mystery and delight.

These coming-of-age rituals were ours to design and develop as parents. As grandparents, our role is different. Owen turned ten in 2021, and we are thinking ahead about how to mark his coming of age. Before Stuart and I plan anything, however, we need to check in with both his parents and his Grandma Nancy (sadly, Granddad Clayton died in 2021). We don't want to do anything that interferes or conflicts with the family plans to honor the thirteenth birthday, and we don't want to set a precedent of more and more elaborate plans. We want to not stand out but rather fit in to a larger plan. The key will be good conversations with parents and the other grandparent and then with Owen himself over the course of the next three years.

One of the fun ways to plan for this momentous stage of life is to read about it and watch movies together. From the earliest literature, we have stories about boys becoming men and girls becoming women, undergoing tests and trials. In *The Odyssey*, we meet young Telemachus and Mentor, the character who lends his name to one of the many roles that grandparents can occupy. *Huckleberry Finn*, *Great Expectations*, *A Tree Grows in Brooklyn*, *Catcher in the Rye*, *Little Women*, *To Kill a Mockingbird*, and *I Know Why the Caged Bird Sings* are classics in the genre. More recent examples include *Roll of Thunder, Hear My Cry*, *The Hate U Give*, and *How the Garcia Girls Lost Their Accents*.

Movies are a wonderful way to invite conversation about coming of age. In addition to giving us narratives and characters to talk about with our grandchildren, we can invite them to popcorn and a movie night or watch simultaneously using one of many apps designed for that purpose. (There are easy online instructions for watching movies with long-distance friends.) Here are a few titles appropriate for tweens: *E.T. the Extra-Terrestrial*, *Stand by Me*, and *My Girl*. Many Disney and Pixar movies focus on coming of age: *Moana*, *The Little Mermaid*, *The Lion King*, *Toy Story*, *Pinocchio*, and *Bambi*, for example. Various websites offer long lists of coming-of-age books and films. As you look at such lists, you will have to be intentional about questions of gender and race because, often, the "classics" listed are created by and about white males. Anne Moody's *Coming of Age in Mississippi* and *Brown Girl Dreaming* by Jacqueline Woodson are splendid coming-of-age stories by women of color.

In addition to reading books and watching films, we can design rituals akin to those of other cultures and times. A coming-of-age ritual that derives from Native American cultures, the vision quest, involves three stages: preparation, solo, return. I look forward to telling Owen about the hawk that visited me during a quest a few decades ago.

Nature provides a setting appropriate for wonder and curiosity, essential ingredients of ritual. If camping has been a part of your family life, you might design a special coming-of-age camping experience. Together you might ponder what the trees and caves, birds, and bees teach us about growing up.

I wonder what our young adult grandchildren will ask us—and what they will teach us—about who we are and who we are called to become. The conversation is, of course, what grandparenting, and life itself, is all about.

Suggestions for Grandparents

1. In addition to the many books and films mentioned in this chapter, books about ritual itself might be helpful. I recommend *The Four-Fold Way* by Angeles Arrien and the TEDx Talk she gave in 2013. *The Power of Ritual: Turning Everyday Activities into Soulful Practices* by Casper ter Kuile describes how to make ritual a part of daily life through another three-step process: set an intention, pay attention, repeat.

2. Ask your friends how they mark special occasions in the lives of their grandchildren. Social media is a great place to crowdsource ideas in a short amount of time.

3. Some grandparents offer to take each grandchild on a trip, to a destination the grandchild chooses, to mark a special birthday. Perhaps the child has shown serious interest in the place, and together the grandparents and grandchild can study the place in advance and document their trip afterward. Road Scholar offers a wide range of group tours for children ages nine to twelve and their grandparents. They look like great fun!

52

THE WORLD THEY GET

Marilyn

World as it is, / what's strong and separate falters.
—John Ciardi, "Most like an Arch This Marriage"

Skye, our youngest grandchild, was born on the other side of the continent in the first year of the pandemic. We will be meeting her for the first time in person just before she turns one. We have rejoiced from afar, celebrated her as we can, and had many moments of poignant pleasure watching her take in the world around her, still so vast and beautiful and new. It is also a world whose conflicts and challenges she will learn about soon enough, and whose troubled history she will inherit.

It's always the case that children are born into a paradox—a shadowed "vale of tears," on the one hand, and a world lined with sunlight and flowers and breathtaking beauty. It's now the case in new ways.

There's a time to push to the background all the hard stuff and just snuggle the baby. Certainly the day she arrives home is one of those times. And beyond that, birthdays, baptisms, learning to jump rope, the first visit from the tooth fairy, starting school: these are times to savor the present.

There's also a time, I think, to step back from the sweetness of the little smiles and sleepy times and admiration of tiny feet to widen our sense of what we as elders are about. In these times, we can assess the sobering task of preparing children for the world they get. The task puts us, as well as them, on a new learning curve. And not one with an even or predictable trajectory. As I've learned to tell students, "You never know what you're being prepared for."

The world they get will be significantly different from our world.

They get a world in which remote virtual connection is both normative and vulnerable. The virtual connectedness we have come to depend on for everything—from family visits during quarantine to daily news updates—will be a constant feature of their lives. They will learn keyboarding skills at the same time as (or possibly before) they learn to print their names. They will expect and receive instant answers to questions—not always authoritative but always available. That this lifeline can be hacked is a background threat they and their parents will live with the way many of us lived with the Cold War.

They get a world in which institutions are in profound transition. The ways education, health care, and other social services, music, art, and voting are accessed will likely be different, possibly in good ways. There may be more fluidity and choice. There may be more local variation. There will certainly be more access to what once could only be gained by travel or by hours in library stacks. (I already miss the library stacks, even though, on any given day, it's easier to do my research on-screen.)

They get a world in which the generational divide is greater than it was for us or for our parents. The skill sets they will be expected to develop early will likely be unfamiliar to us. Many of us have already given up the struggle to keep up with Instagram, TikTok, or Snapchat; new methods of learning math; mastery of techno-slang; or tracking the rapidly evolving forms of music and a cast of role models that may seem to change monthly and get younger all the time. Our grandchildren's dinner-table allusions to a current song or source of information will likely be as unfamiliar to us as the Vietnam War or encyclopedia sets are to them.

They get a world in which neighborhoods and interdependence may be redefined in promising ways. A global pandemic and its aftermath may leave us traveling less and walking the streets near home more regularly. We may all become newly aware of the people who live near us because more of them work from home. As food systems struggle, more community gardens may bring people together and help us retrieve a relationship to the earth and one another. We may once again be learning to love the ones we're with when we can't be with the ones we love.

Our grandchildren get a world in which global awareness will have to develop early. They'll have to learn to cope with an information flow that has multiplied exponentially and continues to do so. They will need, for new reasons, to understand how they're connected to children working in factories in Indonesia or studying in classrooms in China or learning to survive in war zones.

They get a world in which tolerance of violence has risen steadily. What they see even during closely supervised screen time will not be free of it. We will be involved in helping them retain or revive moral sensitivities that are easily eroded.

This may sound unnecessarily dismal. Yet the difficulties their generation faces may help them widen their vision, be intentional about their moral and faith commitments, and develop resilience and social awareness. They may grow up with new strengths and new ways of understanding themselves as global citizens on a journey together. They may be energized by those challenges rather than disheartened. We may see a generation of children more like Greta Thunberg or Malala Yousafzai or X González or Asean Johnson—children who learn early to speak up for those who suffer and for the earth they are inheriting.

As our grandchildren's awareness grows, we will be standing in the widening circle of elders around them, offering encouragement and comfort where we can, occasional applause, and a bit of historical perspective or guidance. We may not be able to make their lives simpler or altogether safer, but we can make sure they know that on this earthly adventure they will be held, witnessed, accompanied, and loved.

Suggestions for Grandparents

1. Many sources of ongoing education can keep us clued in to global realities. From open classes at community colleges, to online courses by major universities, to the amazing array of how-to videos, there's virtually no end to what we can keep learning. Educating ourselves not only helps us stay in conversation with the kids in our lives; it fosters our own life-giving curiosity and investment in the world we share with them while we're all here.

2. Consider providing occasional "countercultural" experiences for your grandchildren—a totally nonelectronic sleepover, for instance, or making up a board game and playing it. Or you could simply tell stories that remind them not just what earlier times were like but what pleasure might still be reintroduced and enjoyed with a little rearrangement of expectations. We can connect our grandchildren to a usable past. Our job is to make it not only usable but "user-friendly."

ACKNOWLEDGMENTS

I want to pay tribute here especially to my own mother, Mary, and grandmother, Effie, both of whose love, wisdom, lively sense of humor, and watchful eyes have served me well since my childhood in our three-generation household. I continue to call on their guidance.

I'm grateful, too, for dear friends who have shared their own adventures in grandparenting over the past several years, especially Kathryn Reiss, Anne Hawkins, Cherla Leonardini, Norma Brunsell, Marilea Wolf, and Meg O'Neill, and to the other women who share that role with me as we watch the children we love grow into their own lives—Pat Taylor, Nancy Teichert, Galina Kaganovich, Joan Petrick, and Cecilia Griffith. I continue to learn from each of them about the love that has "a thousand faces."

I'm also grateful for the wonderful grandfathers in my life—my own, my children's, and my grandchildren's (Jack Chandler, LeGare Chandler, Henry Teichert, Fred Teichert, and, every day, John McEntyre, my spouse, cograndparent, first reader, and generous encourager)—for the love they've given the children we love.

And many thanks to Valerie Weaver-Zercher for her thoughtful, patient editing and encouragement.

—*Marilyn*

My mother, Barbara Ann Hershey Becker, is my living connection to the generations before me and has lavished love on all her thirteen grandchildren and twenty-one great-grandchildren.

My writing group, Powderhorse, provided much encouragement: Jennifer Murch, Jim Clemens, Carolyn Yoder, Valerie Serrels, and Ted Swartz. I also wish to thank Wicked Grace book club members Joanne Gabbin, Linda Thomas-Mobley, Casonya Johnson, Jennifer Davis Sensenig, Amanda Gookin, Bethany Nowviskie, Sofia Samatar, Diane Phoenix-Neal, Louise Hostetler, and Lisa Alleyne. Casonya Johnson was interviewed for this book in chapter 49.

Three college friends, Mary Fretz, Tina Glanzer, and Gloria Rosenberger, have been sharing grandmother wisdom with me for the last eleven years. Gloria's story appears in chapter 44. So many other grandmothers, too numerous to mention, have shared stories that influenced me. Special thanks to Joan Kauffman, interviewed chapter 48. Carol Bodensteiner read the text and provided insightful comments.

My two "pilgrim sisters," Janet Guthrie and Anne Ponder, started out as professional friends (former college presidents) and have become much more. Both grandmothers now, they have taught me much about how complex and creative today's intergenerational families are.

I, too, wish to thank Valerie Weaver-Zercher, editor extraordinaire. And always, I thank Stuart Showalter, my partner in life, and Granddad to our beloved little ones.

—*Shirley*